AF262905

CURSED!

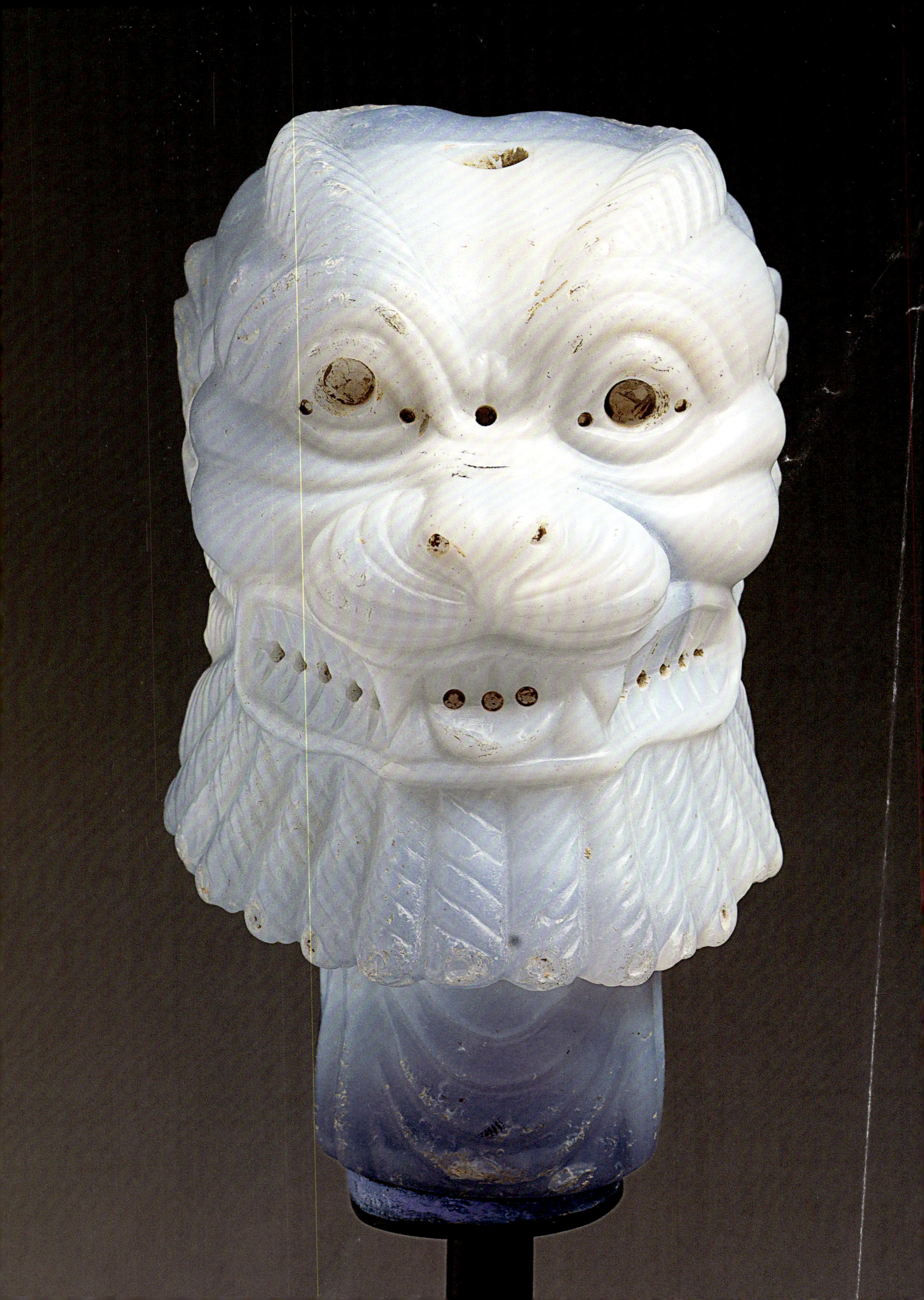

CURSED!

The Power of Magic in the Ancient World

Jeffrey Spier

with contributions by

Gina Konstantopoulos

and Foy Scalf

TOLEDO MUSEUM OF ART

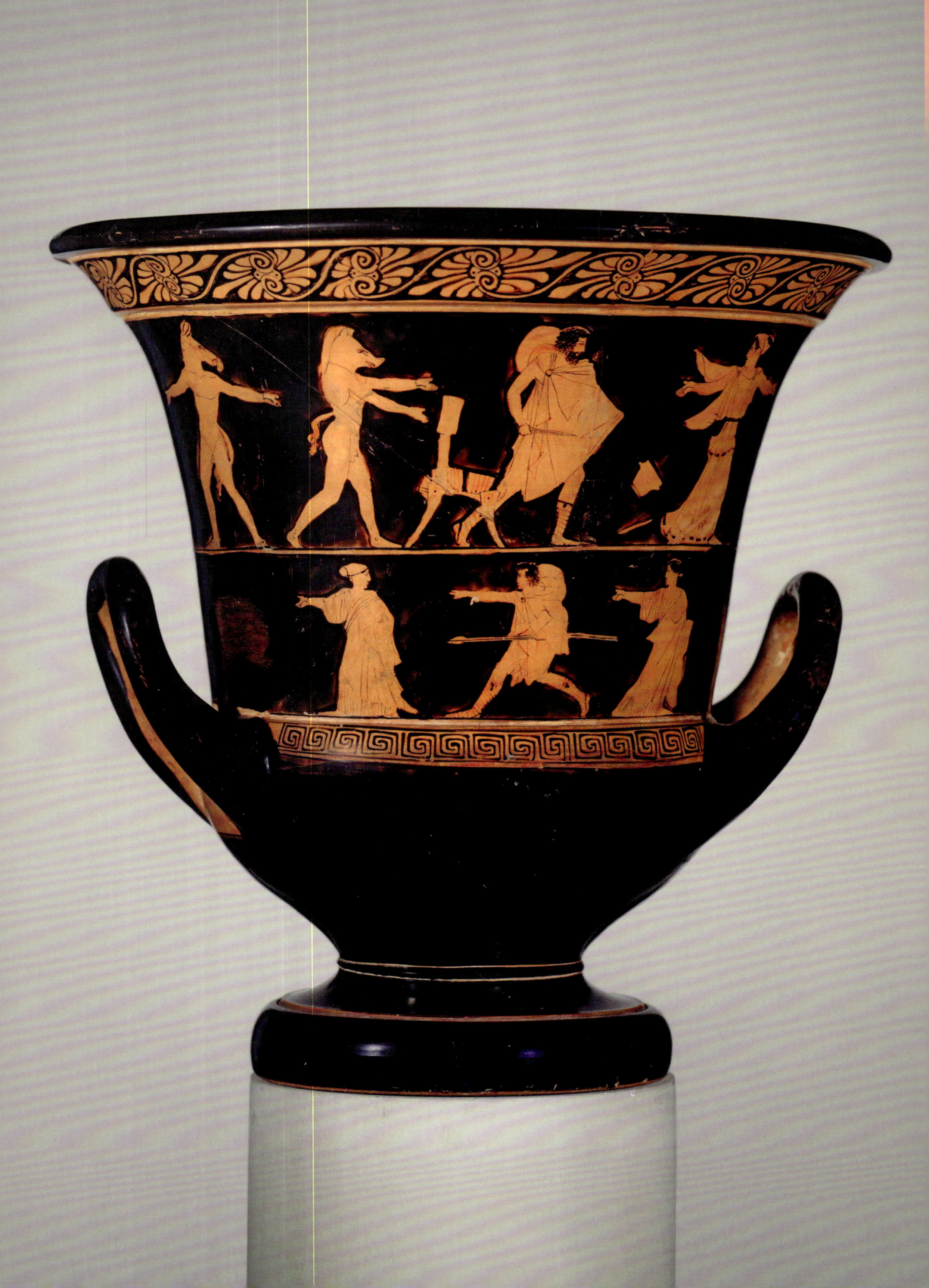

Contents

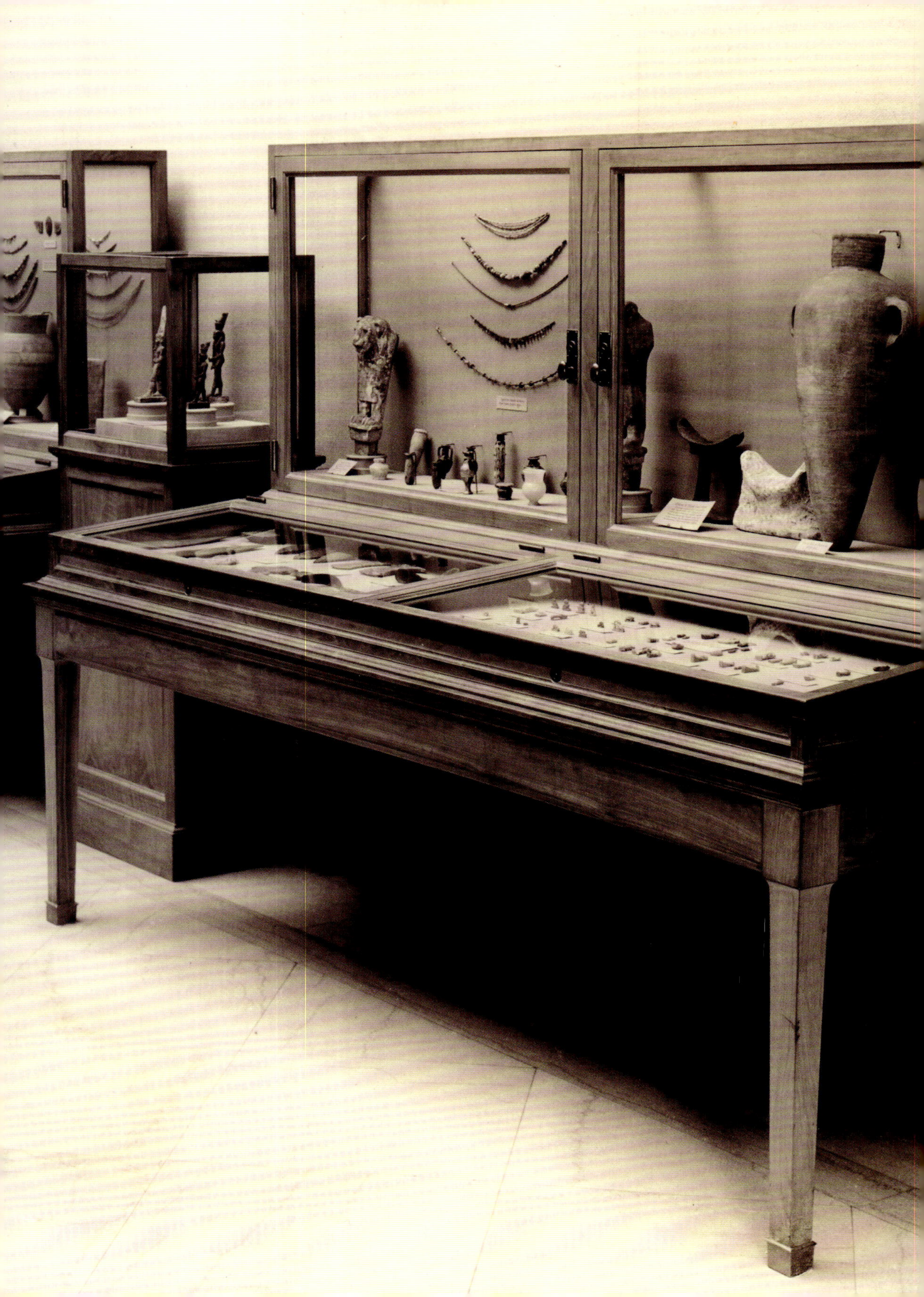

Director's Foreword

ADAM M. LEVINE

Edward Drummond and Florence Scott Libbey President, Director, and CEO

AT THE HEART of many ancient magical traditions lies a deceptively simple idea: If we just say the right words in the right order, if we follow the proper ritual, if we wear or bury or break the right object—then, perhaps, things will finally go our way. This promise of transformation, of control amid chaos, is what makes ancient magic feel both so distant and so familiar. A group of Egyptian amulets collected by Edward Drummond Libbey and Florence Scott Libbey during their 1906 trip to Egypt, some of the earliest works to enter the Toledo Museum of Art's collection, attests to this enduring fascination with magical objects and their power (fig. 1).

Cursed! The Power of Magic in the Ancient World invites visitors to explore a world in which magic was not illusion or sleight of hand but a vital tool for navigating daily life. Spanning more than two millennia and drawing on traditions from Mesopotamia, Egypt, Greece, and Rome, this exhibition reveals how individuals and communities sought to protect the vulnerable, heal the body, hex adversaries, and even influence the divine.

Cursed! brings works of exceptional visual interest and intellectual significance to Toledo. Ivory wands, apotropaic amulets, magical papyri, and curse tablets illuminate how magic functioned in dialogue (and sometimes in tension) with religion, medicine, and law. These objects blur boundaries that may feel rigid today: between religion and science, medicine and spirituality, public practice and private need. In doing so, they offer us a new lens through which to understand how people in the ancient world faced suffering and desire. They also reveal how greatly perceptions of magic could vary, from the state-sponsored rituals of Egyptian temple priests to the

FIG. 1
Amulets on view in a case in TMA's Egyptian Gallery, after 1933

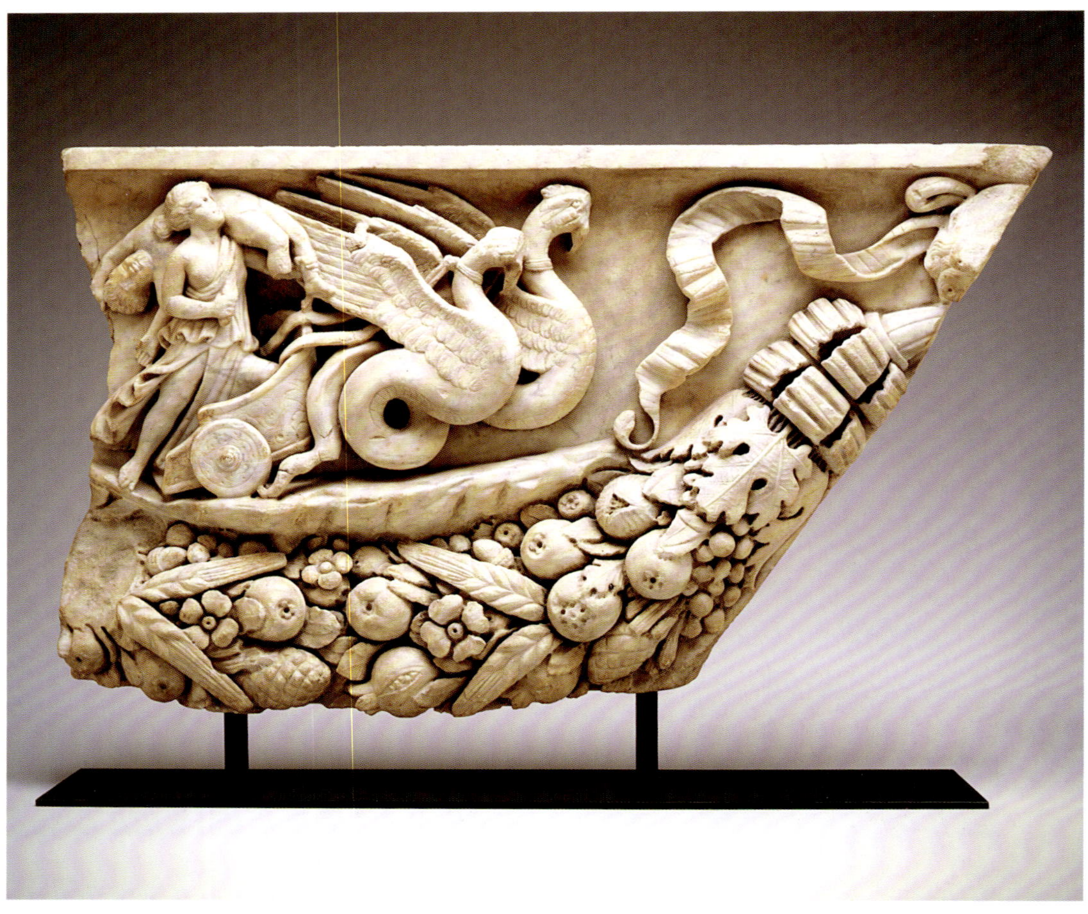

illicit acts attributed to foreign sorcerers in the Greco-Roman world—perhaps none more famous than the murderous Medea (fig. 2).

While we like to believe that the Toledo Museum of Art has always been a magical place to visit, this exhibition makes that feeling literal. We strive to create exhibitions that not only advance scholarship but resonate with our visitors, connecting the past with the present in meaningful, sometimes unexpected ways. *Cursed!* fulfills this purpose by encouraging us to reconsider the boundaries we often draw between belief and skepticism, tradition and invention, or ritual and reason.

Cursed! is the result of years of sustained research and collaboration. We are especially grateful to Dr. Jeffrey Spier, whose scholarly vision and long-standing commitment to this material have shaped the exhibition and this publication. We also extend our deepest thanks to the many institutions whose generosity in lending key objects has made this project possible, including the Biblioteca Medicea Laurenziana, Florence, and Director Francesca Gallori; the Bibliothèque nationale de France, President Gilles Pécout, and Mathilde Avisseau-Broustet; the British Museum, Director Nicholas Cullinan, Daniel Antoine, Paul Collins, and Thomas Harrison; the Brooklyn Museum, Director Anne Pasternak, and Elizabeth Largi; the J. Paul Getty Museum, Director Timothy Potts, Sara Cole, and David Saunders; the Johns Hopkins Archaeological Museum and Director Dr. Betsy M. Bryan; the Kelsey Museum of Archaeology at the University of Michigan, Director Nicola Terrenato, and Michelle Fontenot; the Metropolitan Museum of Art, CEO and Director Max Hollein, Séan Hemingway, and Adela Oppenheim; the Musée du Louvre, President and Director Laurence des Cars, and Ariane Thomas; the Musées royaux d'Art et d'Histoire / Koninklijke Musea voor Kunst en Geschiedenis, Brussels, General Director Géraldine David, and Natacha Massar; the Petrie Museum of Egyptian and Sudanese Archaeology at University College London and Catriona Wilson; the Special Collections Research Center at the University of Michigan Library, Director Martha O'Hara Conway, and Pablo Alvarez; the Walters Art Museum, Executive Director and CEO Kate Burgin, Mary Cochran, and Christine Sciacca; and the Wyvern Research Institute, London, Chair Sir Paul Ruddock, and Director Susannah Kingwill. Special thanks are due to Maria Cristina White da Cruz for her untiring assistance.

In the ancient world, magic offered not just answers, but agency. It was a way to act—to hope, to intervene, to heal. This impulse has not vanished. It lingers in the way we grasp for meaning, protection, or reassurance, especially in moments of uncertainty. We hope this exhibition inspires visitors to see the ancient world with renewed clarity and to recognize within it the deep human desire to make sense of forces larger than ourselves.

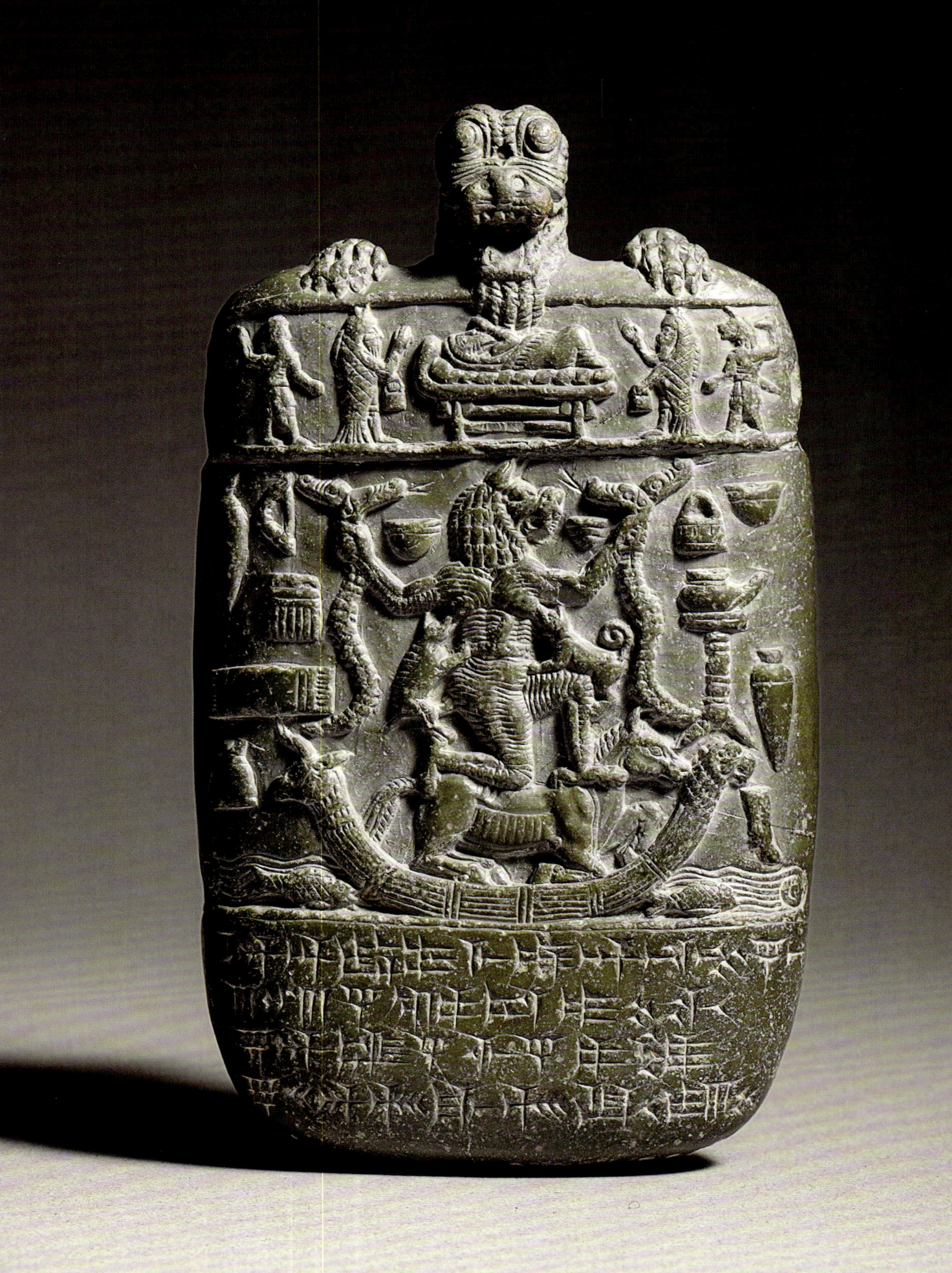

Magic

JEFFREY SPIER

WHAT IS MAGIC? The meaning of the word is controversial and varies
from culture to culture, but in its most basic form, *magic* refers to the
belief that individuals have the power to manipulate nature (as well
as their fellow human beings) by means of rituals that make use of
particular materials—whether animal, plant, or mineral—and the
recitation or writing of secret names and spells that call on divinities
for assistance. These magical acts were intended to achieve a variety
of goals, ranging from mystical enlightenment to protecting individuals from demonic harm, curing medical ailments, cursing adversaries,
securing lovers, affecting the outcomes of legal disputes, and many
others.

Those who performed such acts were often priests or other
representatives of conventional religion, but they may also have been
society's outsiders—those called magicians, sorcerers, or witches. In
pharaonic Egypt and ancient Mesopotamia, rituals that in later times
would be considered magic were very much part of official religion.
Priests in Egypt provided medical cures, often including the recitation of spells, which were detailed in books passed down over
generations; they provided amulets for protection; and, on behalf
of the pharaoh, they performed execration (cursing) rituals that
involved the smashing of clay figurines representing foreign enemies
of the state. As in Egypt, priests in Babylon were part of the religious
establishment under the jurisdiction of the king. They, too, performed healing rituals and made amulets to protect individuals. They
were also responsible for keeping demonic forces away from the city
by carefully following the complex *Maqlû* ritual, which was inscribed
on a series of clay tablets.

None of these rituals would have been considered improper in Egypt or Mesopotamia, but in Greece and Rome, similar activities were viewed with suspicion and usually disapproval. Practitioners of magic were not sanctioned religious figures but often foreigners with questionable intentions—most famously represented by the mysterious and powerful foreign sorceresses of Greek myth, Circe and Medea. Actual foreign magicians were visiting Greece by the fifth century BCE, but plenty of Greeks, too, took part in these activities. Although educated, upper-class Greeks typically expressed the view that purported magicians were impious, unethical, or just frauds, magical practices proliferated. Curses and love charms written on lead tablets became common and were apparently readily available for purchase.

Following Alexander the Great's conquest of the eastern Mediterranean and the Persian Empire at the end of the fourth century BCE, a wide variety of magical traditions—Egyptian, Babylonian, Persian, Jewish, and others—became known to the Greeks, especially in the newly founded and highly cosmopolitan city of Alexandria in Egypt. Soon afterward, the same magical practices spread throughout the Roman Empire. Although Greek and Roman literature relates that magic continued to be considered a disreputable practice and was sometimes even illegal, traces of its existence can be found throughout Europe, North Africa, and the Middle East, from Egypt to England.

Cursed! The Power of Magic in the Ancient World brings together archaeological evidence of magical practices in the ancient Mediterranean region. We begin with Egyptian rituals performed by official priests, including cursing and healing, and continue with the texts used by Babylonian ritual specialists to perform exorcisms of witchcraft and demons. Moving on to Greece, we encounter the sorceresses Circe, who transformed men into animals until the hero Odysseus learned how to counteract her magic, and Medea, who was skilled with magic potions that could either heal or kill. Evidence for early Greek magical practices is found in the use of curse tablets and doll-like figures that represented the victims.

The new form of magic that emerged at the end of the first century BCE, which might be termed "international magic" for its multicultural character and widespread use, is documented by actual books of magical rituals and spells written on papyrus that were discovered in Egypt. A variety of amulets came into use as well, including not only curses and love charms written on lead but others written on gold and silver that served for protection or as medical cures. Amulets finely carved from semiprecious stone with depictions of strange deities and inscribed with magic words in Greek became especially popular.

Although *Cursed!* concludes in the third century CE, these magical practices did not. Belief in magic and the passing down of spells and rituals continued, even with the rise of Christianity and Islam, and many of these traditions survive today. *Abracadabra* is a magic word first attested in a medical spell written down by the Roman physician Quintus Serenus Sammonicus around the year 200 CE, but it remains well known to us all.

Magic in Ancient Egypt

FOY SCALF

FOR MILLENNIA, Egypt has been synonymous with magic. Biblical texts, Greek and Roman authors, and Renaissance scholars all portrayed the Egyptians as master magicians. From the Old Testament's sorcerers to the enigmatic Hermes Trismegistus (an avatar of the god Thoth), Egypt's magical traditions captured the imaginations of outsiders.[1] But how did the Egyptians themselves understand magic? What we call magic today encompasses a range of practices that, in ancient Egypt, were fundamental aspects of religion rather than illicit or marginal activities. From our modern perspective, there are beliefs and practices that we can group together under our use of the term "magic," although only from an outsider's perspective, as there is no one-to-one correlation with an ancient Egyptian concept. In general, what binds these diverse cultural traits together is a belief that humans can influence the course of events in their lives by taking agency.

At the heart of Egyptian magical practice was *heka*, often translated as "magic."[2] More than spells or rituals, heka was a fundamental force of creation, woven into the fabric of the universe. It functioned much like the principle of causality—linking intention and effect—but was inseparable from the divine realm.[3] Thus, heka was embedded in a theological framework that included divine beings and personifications of natural forces. From this point of view, the personified creative force was considered a god (fig. 1), whose name, Heka, was derived from the same word and could be invoked as an agent of causative change.[4]

Ancient Egyptians incorporated what we see as magical practices into nearly all aspects of their lives: day-to-day chores, treatments for

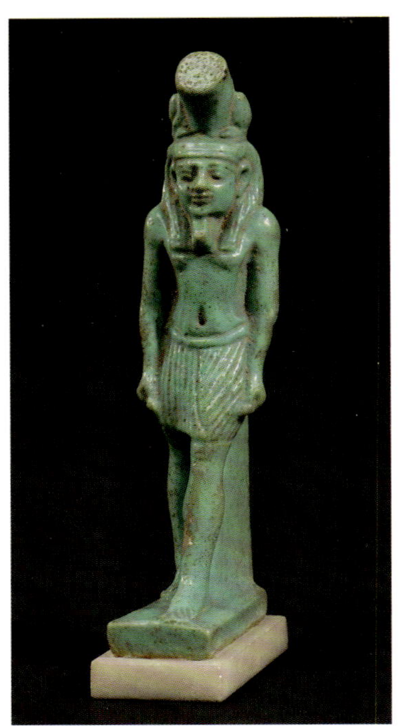

sickness, childcare, protective measures to ward off threats, attempts to find a lover, support for deceased ancestors, ways to propitiate the gods, and methods to ensure the continued existence and function of the universe. To the ancient Egyptians, these practices were a natural part of life. Magic was not a marginal activity; it was an expected part of daily affairs. Magical actions were normal, even required, for all social classes. Children and parents could repeat a spell to help ease the pain of a scorpion's sting, priests performed daily rituals to ensure the sanctity of temple spaces, and pharaohs routinely reenacted the triumph of creation over chaos in performative actions of state—most explicitly in the defeat of Egypt's enemies. Our most prolific evidence for the practice of magic in ancient Egypt derives from contexts for assuaging anxieties or treating matters of health, healing, protection, and death, largely filtered through the lens of the literate scribes whose texts bear witness to magic's pervasiveness across the millennia.

In the healing arts, practitioners had all avenues of treatment available to them, including using magical spells and calling on the powers of the gods. The concepts of medicine and magic were not discrete from the ancient Egyptian point of view. The famous Papyrus Ebers (fig. 2), often celebrated as a medical manuscript, begins with a general magical formula: "Beginning with the spell of applying a prescription to any body part of a person." There follows an incantation, which includes a postscript with an enthusiastic endorsement: "Recitation when applying a prescription to any body part of a sick man. Truly effective, millions of times." Two additional spells coincided with the removal of bandages and consuming medicinal drinks. These generic spells were meant to accompany any medical treatments performed by the doctor as detailed in the remaining cases from the Papyrus Ebers reference book. Practitioners and patients alike often performed such recitations over amulets (figs. 3, 4) to further charge them with potential healing properties. Specific amulets, such as the eye of Horus (fig. 5), serve as hieroglyphic symbols for healing itself.[5]

Best exemplifying the inherent power of the written word and iconographic images to endow substances with potency are the so-called magical healing statues. These statues were covered head to toe in texts and images of ritual power. The hieroglyphs often incorporate historiolae—brief mythological narratives—describing

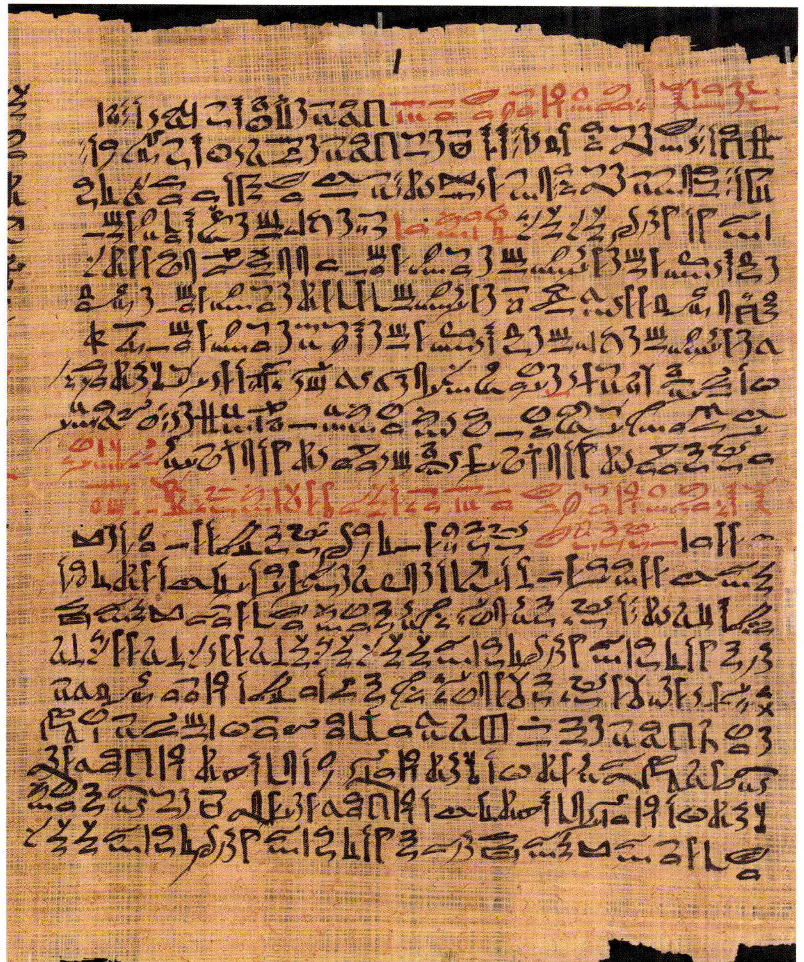

miraculous healings that pilgrims and sufferers sought to replicate. One of the most popular of these myths told the story of the child-god Horus, who was poisoned by snakebite and scorpion sting when his mother Isis hid him amid the marshes to protect him from his uncle Seth, who sought control of Egypt after the death of Horus's father, Osiris.[6] Finding Horus suffering and near death, Isis called out, and the god Thoth came to help revive Horus through a series of incantations. Anyone wanting to avoid suffering such a calamity or who wanted Horus's miraculous healing applied to their ailment could visit a statue inscribed with this story, pour water over the

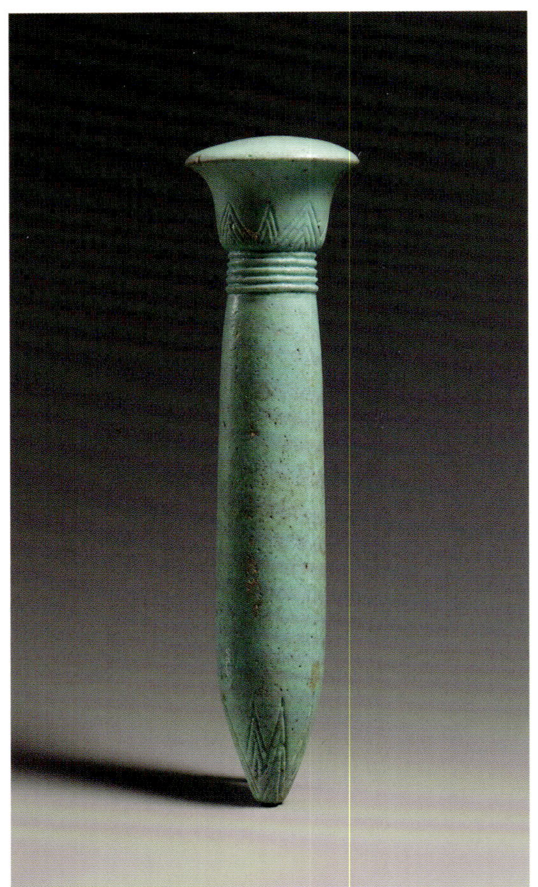

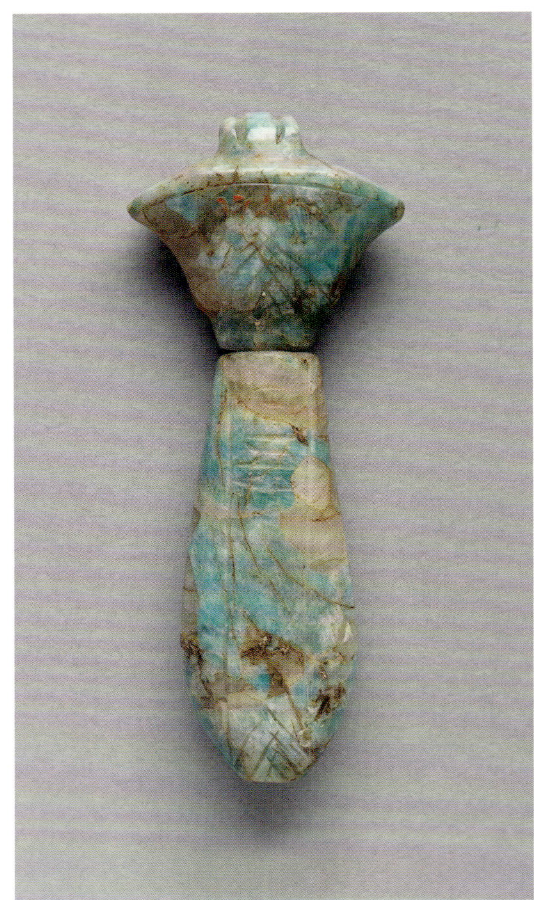

FIG. 3
Papyrus column amulet,
664–332 BCE

FIG. 4
Papyrus column amulet,
about 664–525 BCE

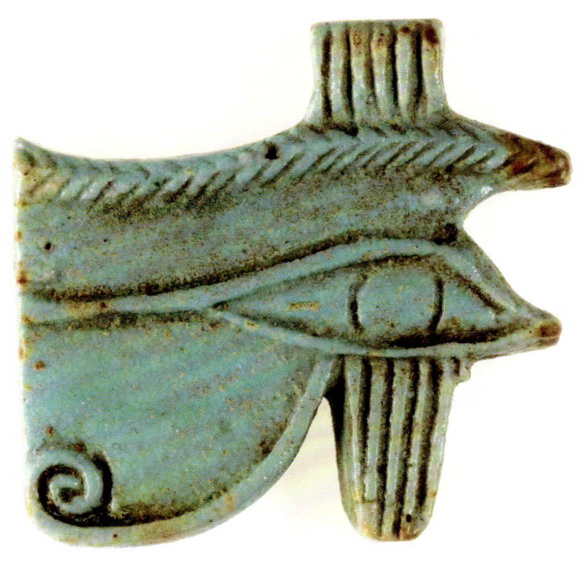

FIG. 5
Wedjat amulet, 664–
332 BCE

FIG. 6
Magical stela of Horus,
360–343 BCE

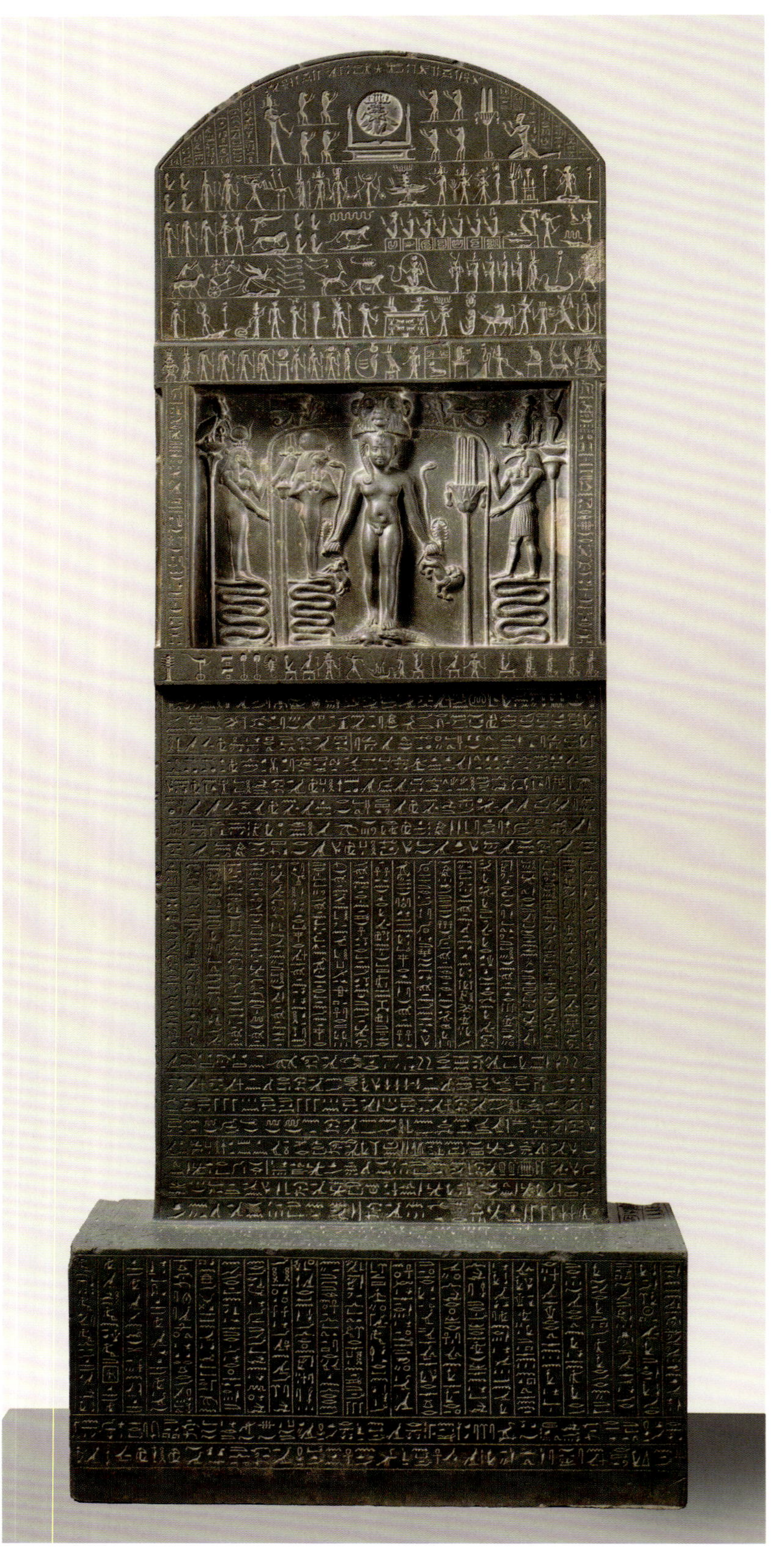

magical texts, and drink the sacred solution empowered with the healing of Horus.[7] An ancient Egyptian priest named Esatum erected the Metternich stela (fig. 6) in memory of his mother; pilgrims would visit the statue in hope of partaking of its restorative waters. Like the central image on the Metternich stela, Padimahes's statue (fig. 7) holds a cippus shrine (an upright, inscribed stela) showing Horus triumphing over the threatening forces of the Egyptian environment: snakes, scorpions, crocodiles, and desert animals. Miniature, handheld examples of these cippi, often referred to as Horus-on-the-Crocodiles stelae, were designed to be carried and dunked in bowls of water or other liquids to transfer their magical healing power (fig. 8).

While heka could be used for protection and healing, it was also a powerful weapon. Egyptian priests and rulers wielded magic to subdue enemies, both human and supernatural. Egyptian magic often relied on sympathetic principles—the belief that objects connected to a person or force could influence them. A lock of hair could be used in a love spell, a figurine could stand in for an enemy, and an inscribed amulet could channel divine protection. By these means, a man could compel a woman to love him through a lock of her hair, or the pain of an illness could be transferred to an object that was summarily destroyed. This magical practice of transference was an apparatus of the Egyptian state; Pharaoh symbolically destroyed Egypt's enemies in large-scale temple scenes depicted throughout the country (fig. 9). In associated execration (curse) rituals, priestly practitioners produced figures of bound captives inscribed with long lists of adversarial names (fig. 10). Participants in the ritual deliberately broke and destroyed the figures in performative acts meant to neutralize and deactivate these individuals' agency in the real world.[8] From Egypt's perspective, such actions could even be seen as motivated by peace, for if Egypt remained an unchallenged superpower, war was superfluous.

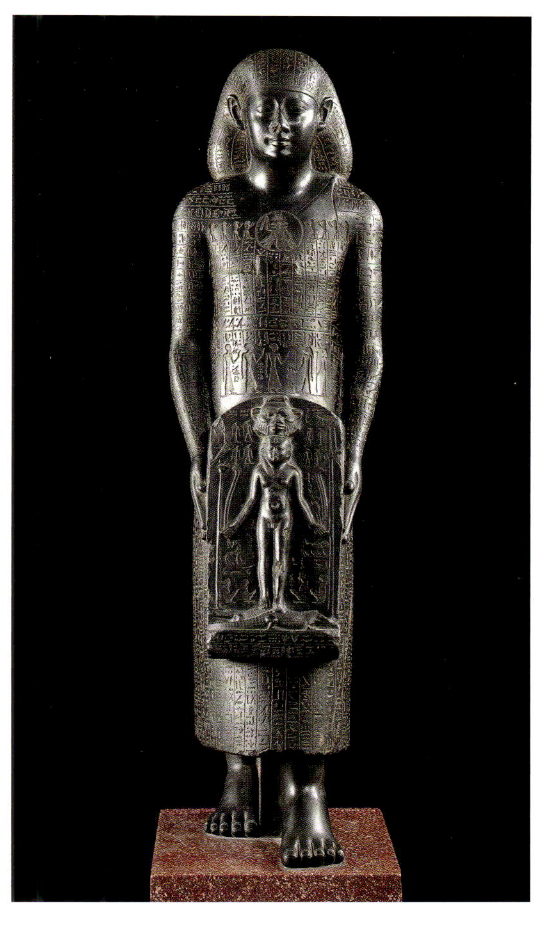

Statue of a priest of Bastet, 4th century BCE

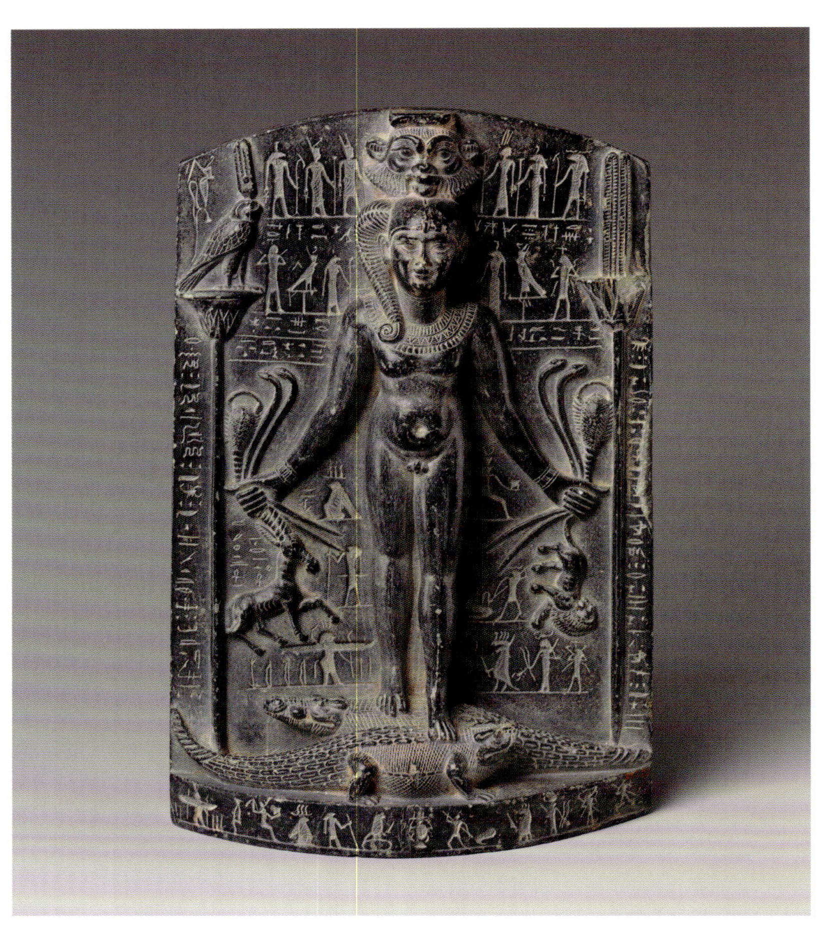

FIG. 8
Magical stela of Horus,
332–280 BCE

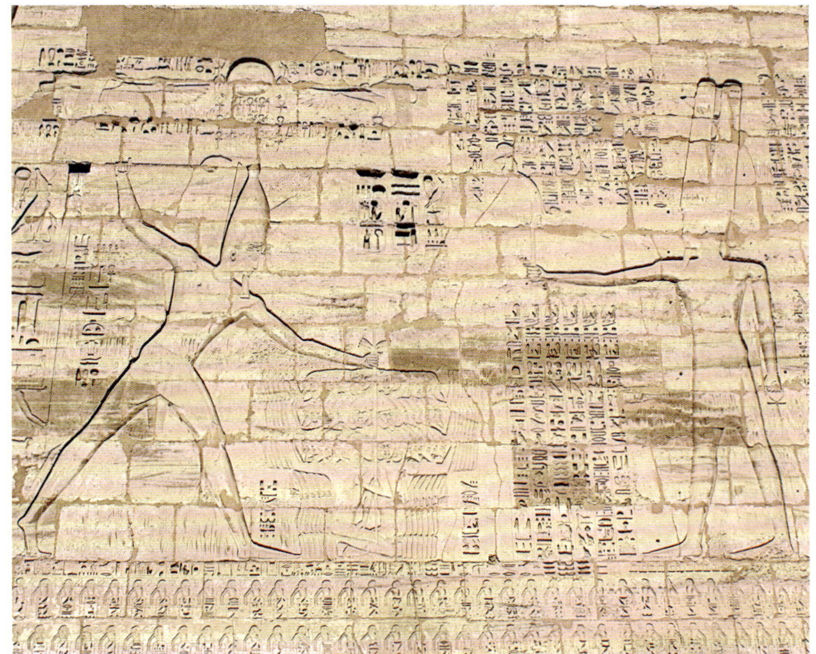

FIG. 9
A scene from the pylon
of Medinet Habu show-
ing Pharaoh Ramses III
smiting enemies before
the god Amun in a per-
formative act meant to
ensure Egypt's security

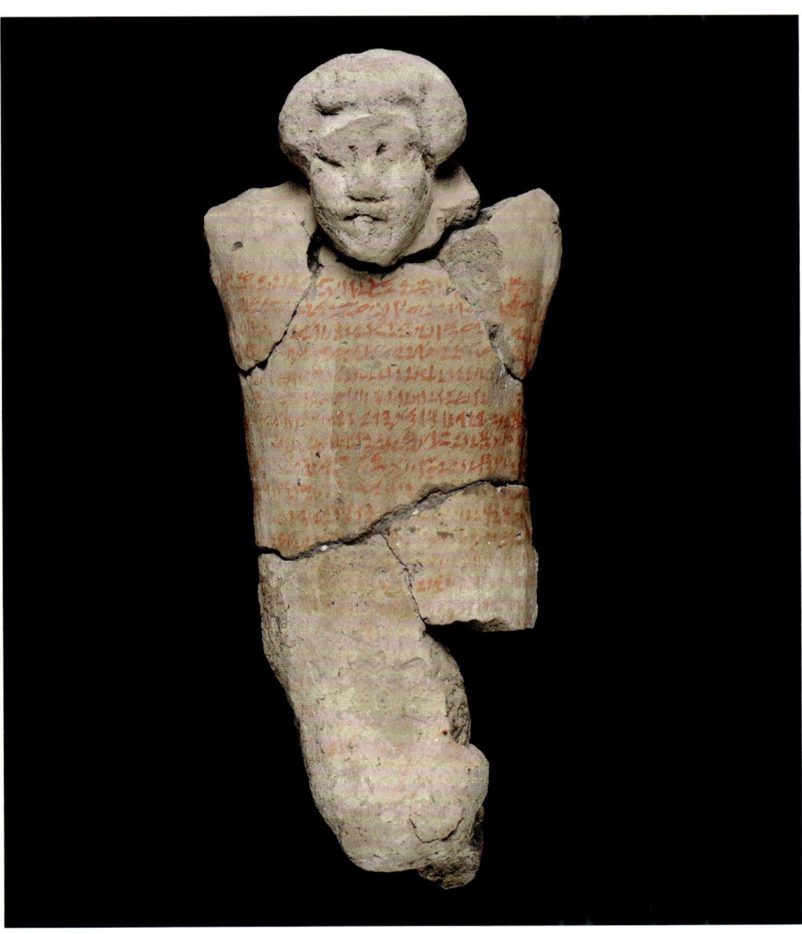

FIG. 10
Curse figure, 1991–
1802 BCE

Execration rites also addressed threatening beings from beyond this world, including the male and female dead. Such lists of threatening beings were adapted from royal rituals and incorporated into many religious and magical spells. An Egyptian artist illustrated one such spell with a polymorphic god described as "Bes with seven faces" (fig. 11), who represented the creator god and his emanations into the world, often referred to in Egyptology as symbolizing the one and the many.[9] All these threats were kept at bay by invoking the power of the collective gods. Yet such invocations reveal an important aspect of ancient Egyptian religious theology: the potential influence of the dead on the world of the living. At the end of life, ancient Egyptians believed that their ancestors became effective spirits called *akhu*, who joined the ranks of the deities in the afterworld, a placed they called the Duat. Like other gods, ancestral spirits had the power to intercede in this life. Family members often wrote letters to their dead relatives asking them for help.[10] Many requests concerned internal family matters: granting of children, assistance in legal matters, support for inheritance, and resolution of disputes. In return, the ancestral spirits were offered support and care in the form of offerings, memorials, and prayers. Some letters were written directly on the bowls or jar stands that held food provisions left in the tomb chapel (fig. 12). Simultaneously, a supplicant could threaten the spirit with lack of sustenance if they refused to act. Such was the ambivalent nature of heka; as a creative force, anyone could wield it against someone else: people toward other people, gods toward gods, and even people toward gods. Antidotes to the attacks of other magicians were common, including spells to repel the evil eye.[11]

Egyptians' destiny as akhu began at their birth. There was a well-developed cottage industry for the protection of women during

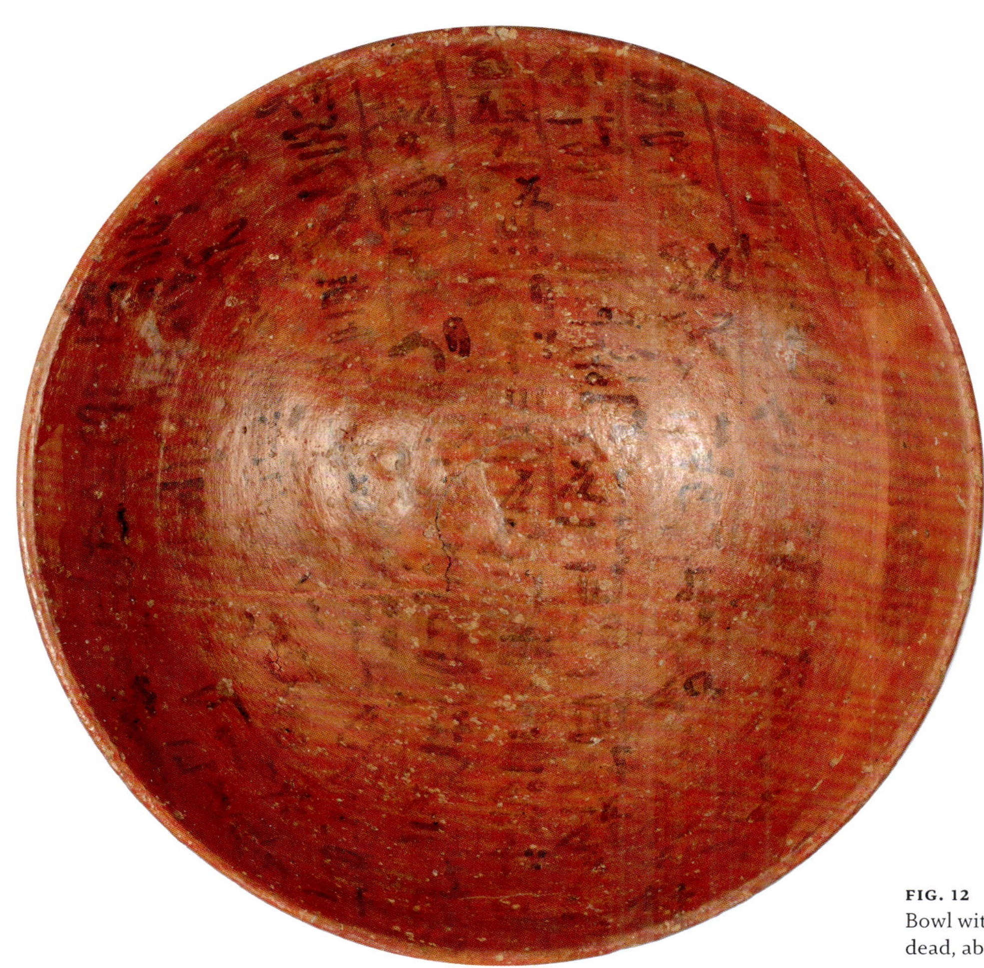

FIG. 12
Bowl with a letter to the
dead, about 2200 BCE

FIG. 13
A papyrus inscribed with
an oracular amuletic
decree of the goddess
Nekhbet promising pro-
tection for Tabakhor
from an extensive list
of possible dangers.
The thin papyrus would
be rolled up and worn
in a small case around
the neck.

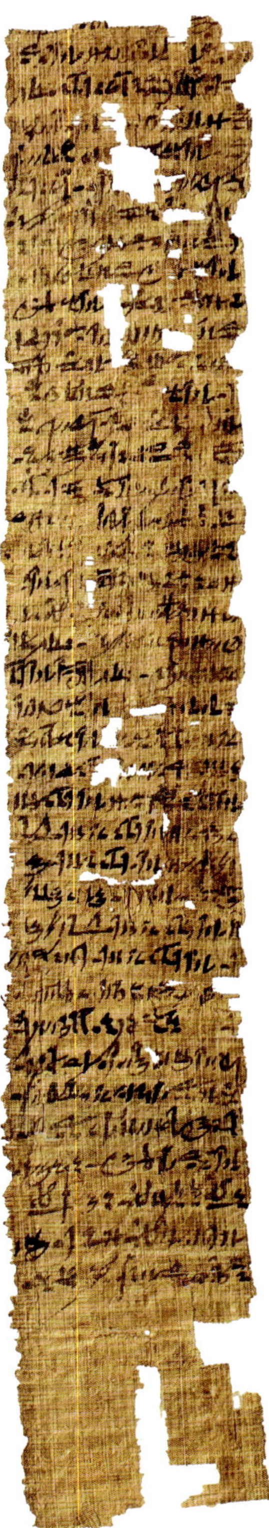
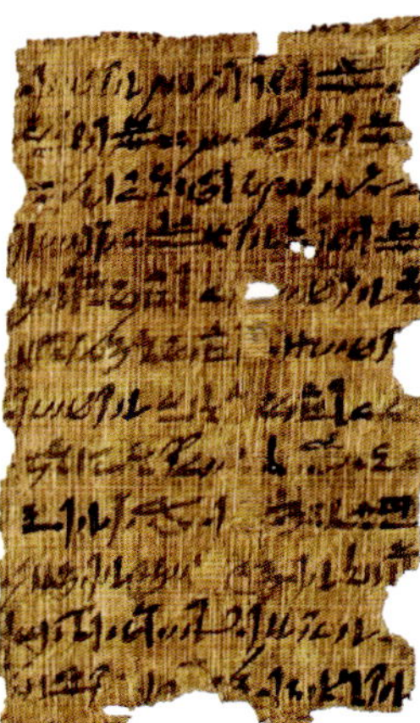
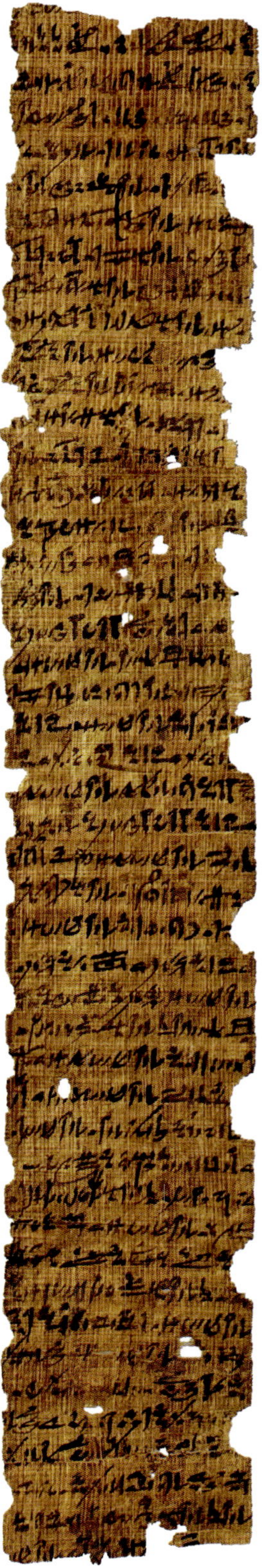

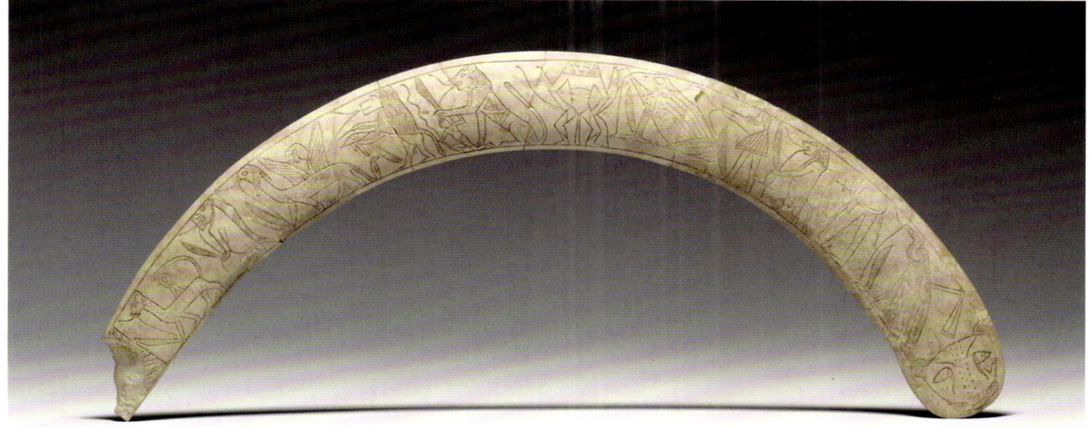

childbirth and care for their resulting children. People commissioned papyri known as oracular amuletic decrees (fig. 13) through temple priests who recorded divine oracles of protection from various gods and goddesses for the commissioner, frequently on behalf of their children. Associated material culture included ivory hippopotamus tusks (fig. 14) carved into a thin crescent shape—often referred to as wands—and engraved with apotropaic symbols. Some symbols consisted of goddesses of childbirth, such as Taweret (fig. 15), depicted as a hippo, who could also be found as a constellation in the northern sky.[12] Inscriptions on selected examples demonstrate clearly that the wands were intended for the safety of recently born children.

For an ancient Egyptian, magic was present at birth, throughout life, and, most famously, all-encompassing at death. Tombs commissioned by the elite population served as magical cocoons, filled with redundant layers of materials, rituals, and spells. Inscriptions often adorned every available surface, from the tomb walls and coffin boards to the linen wrappings and papyri. Likewise, amulets and amuletic figures surrounded the mummified body. A set of magical bricks warded off evil from sockets in the burial chamber walls along the cardinal directions (fig. 16). Gold adornments (fig. 17) were strung around the neck, while networks of amulets adorned the wrappings. Rituals and their associated invocations activated this sacred space and imbued the objects with supranatural energy. If you had the money in ancient Egypt, you could help alleviate your mortal anxiety by taking agency over the unknown and turning to magic as a natural force to make your dreams come true.

FIG. 15
Amulet of Taweret,
664–332 BCE

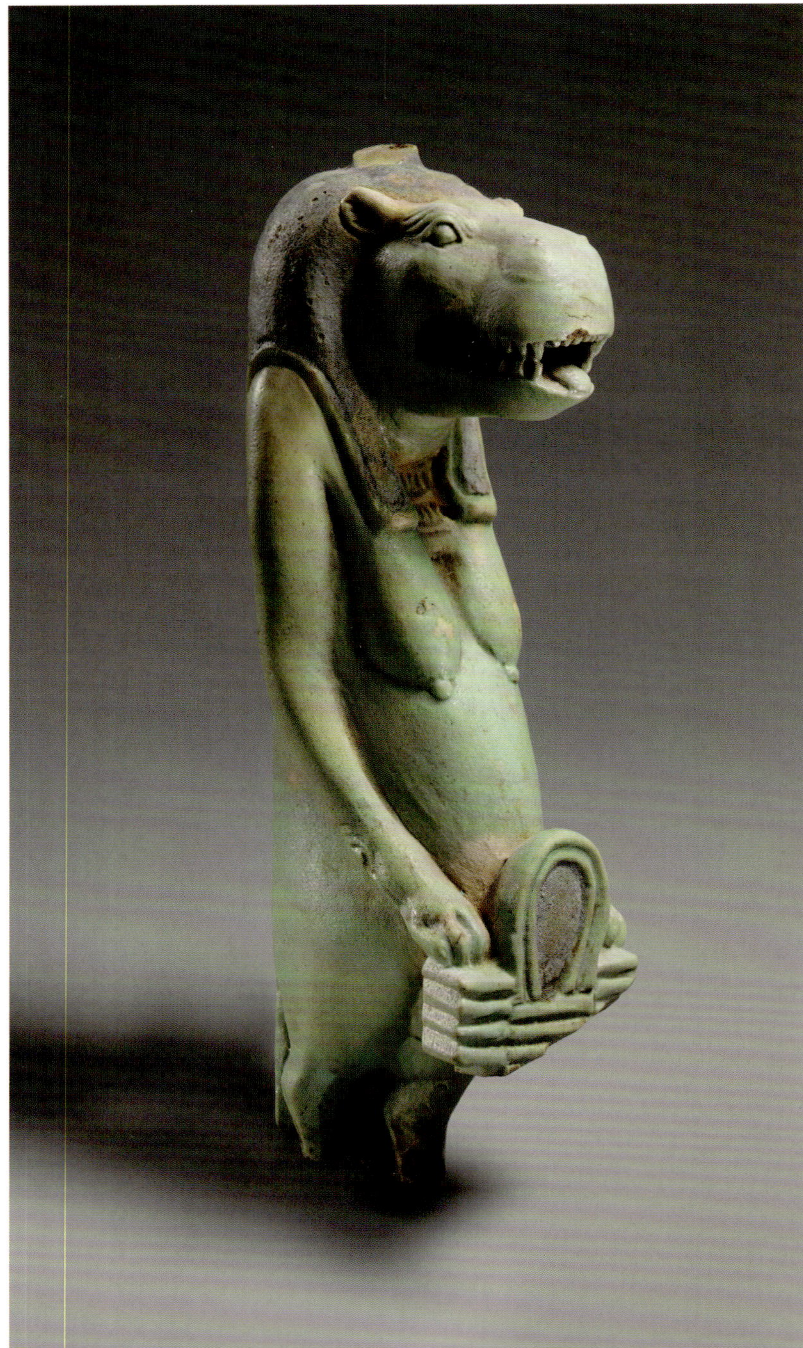

FIG. 16
A group of selected mag-
ical bricks belonging to
different individuals,
inscribed with sections
of Book of the Dead spell
151 to ward off dangers
from the cardinal direc-
tions. Sets were placed
in niches within the
walls of burial chambers.

FIG. 17
Amulets from the burial
of Djedmutesankh,
1000–945 BCE

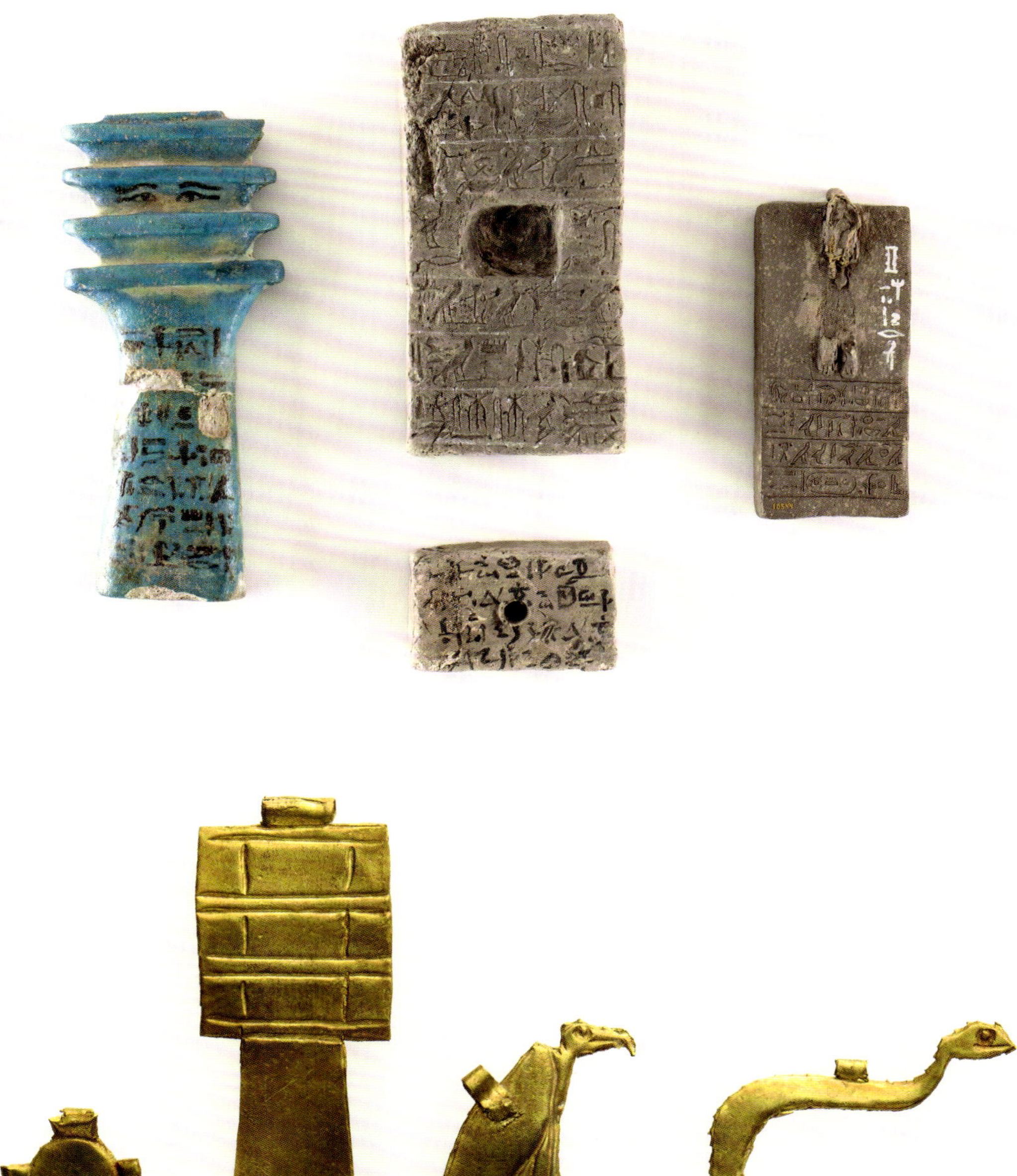

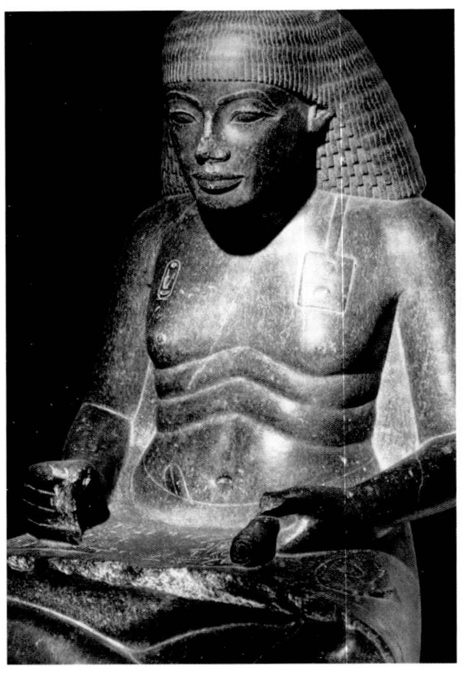

The scribal priest was an important linchpin in helping achieve such dreams by tying all these practices together within a population. Access to literacy was restricted in ancient Egypt; production of texts, particularly those with esoteric religious content, would have required highly trained people. Many ancient Egyptian priests worked on a rotational schedule. When they were off rotation, they had ample time to serve their local communities, particularly for intellectual and literary requirements in the matters of magic, medicine, religion, and law.[13] Their skills often brought them great renown, and particularly important practitioners, such as Amenhotep, son of Hapu, became venerated saints. Their images were imbued with magical healing powers and became centerpieces of worship by pilgrims, whose desire to be healed can still be seen in the smoothed stone of Amenhotep's statue where pilgrims over millennia rubbed off the hieroglyphic text from the papyrus on his lap in hopes of cure and sanctity (fig. 18). Despite the vital role of these scribal priests, it is important to remember that the foundation for all ancient Egyptian magic rested in oral recitation. To that end, members of all social classes regularly participated in magical practices by reciting spells for protection, healing, and the commemoration of their ancestors.

NOTES

1. For a comparison of magical practices across the ancient Mediterranean world, see Foy D. Scalf, "Magic," in *Dictionary of Daily Life in Biblical and Post-Biblical Antiquity,* vol. 3: *I–N,* ed. Edwin M. Yamauchi and Marvin R. Wilson (Hendrickson, 2016), 201–20. For an overview of Egyptian influence in the Renaissance, see Brian Curran, *The Egyptian Renaissance: The Afterlife of Ancient Egypt in Early Modern Italy* (University of Chicago Press, 2007).

2. For an etymological discussion, see Robert Kriech Ritner, *The Mechanics of Ancient Egyptian Magical Practice* (The Oriental Institute of the University of Chicago, 1993), 25. For an overview of ancient Egyptian magic, in addition to Ritner, see Christoffer Theis, *Magie und Raum: Der magische Schutz auserwählter Räume im alten Ägypten nebst einem Vergleich zu angrenzenden Kulturbereichen* (Mohr Siebeck, 2014).

3. For this causative interpretation, see Herman te Velde, "The God Heka in Egyptian Theology," *Jaarbericht Ex Oriente Lux* 21 (1970): 175–86.

4. As a metaphorical pun emblematic of the god's creative abilities, his name is often written with the hieroglyphic sign for "power" (as in fig. 1). See Ritner, *The Mechanics of Ancient Egyptian Magical Practice*, 25–26, 216. For an example of such invocations, see Pyramid Text spell 539: "It is not this Pepy who says this to you, gods. It is Heka who says this to you, gods." For the text, see James P. Allen, *A New Concordance of the Pyramid Texts; vol. 5: PT 539–672* (Brown University, 2013), 5. For grammatical discussion, see Pascal Vernus, "The Diachronic Variations of a Formulaic Expression for Denying and Shifting the Responsibility and the Magical Processes of Thought It Involves—'C'est pas moi…c'est l'autre.,'" *Zeitschrift für ägyptische Sprache und Altertumskunde* 150 (2022): 130–45.

5. For an overview of amulets and their use, see Joachim Friedrich Quack, *Altägyptische Amulette und ihre Handhabung* (Mohr Siebeck, 2022).

6. James P. Allen, *The Art of Medicine in Ancient Egypt* (Yale University Press, 2005), 49–63.

7. Robert Kriech Ritner, "Horus on the Crocodiles: A Juncture of Religion and Magic in Late Dynastic Egypt," in *Religion and Philosophy in Ancient Egypt*, ed. James P. Allen, Jan Assmann, Alan B. Lloyd, Robert Kriech Ritner, and David P. Silverman (Yale University Press, 1989), 103–16.

8. Tara Prakash, *Ancient Egyptian Prisoner Statues: Fragments of the Late Old Kingdom* (Lockwood Press, 2022); Tori L. Finlayson, "Bound Within a Box: Examination of Execration Figurines of the Egyptian Museum in Cairo," *Journal of Egyptian Archaeology* 106, no. 1–2 (2020): 59–74, and "The Concept of Containment in Execration Rituals: A Case Study," in *Ancient Egyptian Rituals Against Enemies*, ed. Carina Kühne-Wespi and Joachim Friedrich Quack (Mohr Siebeck, 2024), 29–51.

9. Erik Hornung, *Conceptions of God in Ancient Egypt: The One and the Many* (Cornell University Press, 1996), and Joachim Friedrich Quack, "The So-Called Pantheos: On Polymorphic Deities in Late Egyptian Religion," *Aegyptus et Pannonia* 3 (2006): 175–90.

10. Julia Hsieh, *Ancient Egyptian Letters to the Dead: The Realm of the Dead Through the Voice of the Living* (Brill, 2022).

11. Susanne Beck, "Who Is Afraid of…? A Spell Against the Evil Eye (pBM EA10563)," *Journal of Egyptian Archaeology* 110, no. 1–2 (2024): 205–11.

12. For connections between the figures engraved on the tusks and asterisms, see Hartwig Altenmüller, "Symbole von Sternen als Zeichen der Apotropaia," *Göttinger Miszellen: Beiträge zur ägyptologischen Diskussion* 263 (2021): 15–26.

13. Ritner, *The Mechanics of Ancient Egyptian Magical Practice*, 232.

Magic in the Ancient Near East

GINA KONSTANTOPOULOS

A NEO-ASSYRIAN cuneiform tablet in the British Museum provides a valuable window into the world of Mesopotamian magic and witch-craft (fig. 1). The well-preserved tablet contains a nearly complete copy of tablet seven of the anti-witchcraft ritual known as *Maqlû* ("the Burning"), dedicated to countering the malevolent actions of the Mesopotamian witch. The title refers to the ultimate goal of burning away the witch and her malignance, carrying her spirit to the heavens for the gods to deal with. This ritual was collated and compiled in the first millennium BCE, and this tablet stands as a particularly fine example of the text. The Akkadian text of the ritual was found at the Assyrian city of Nineveh, where it belonged to the extensive library of Ashurbanipal, who reigned from 669 to 631 BCE as the last great king of the Neo-Assyrian empire.

Throughout the *Maqlû*, the full range of the witch's malignant actions is described, as are the various ways to counter her. At certain points the afflicted person speaks directly, accusing the witch of making a figurine to harm him, which he will attempt to turn against her: "O witch, who has made a figurine of me, who has looked at my form and created my image [...] The sorcery that you have performed against me, I perform against you."[1] The patient's accusations reveal that Mesopotamian magic and witchcraft functioned along funda-mentally sympathetic means, namely, the belief that effecting or altering a representation of a person (such as a figurine) will cascade onto the person themselves. In Mesopotamia, this was accomplished primarily through the creation and manipulation of figurines, whether of the patient or the witch.

When we speak of "Mesopotamian magic," we compress a complex system of beliefs and practices, all influenced by religious and social customs, that existed for well over two millennia. Despite this, some principles remain fairly consistent, such as the use of sympathetic magic, the chaotic danger of the witch, the highly trained nature of the ritual practitioner, the deities he invoked, and the presence of both beneficial and malevolent demonic figures. In Mesopotamia, we must also be certain to include magic as one part of a larger religious landscape—not separate from ritual or religious worship, but connected to it. Even witchcraft, which often worked against the ordered nature of the Mesopotamian universe, was still within this worldview. Nothing—from magic to witchcraft, from gods to demons—would be viewed as supernatural in the modern sense of the term. In light of these connections, scholars have proposed a definition of Mesopotamian magic as an activity involving specific symbolic actions, such as the burning or destruction of figurines, and ritual recitations, all performed by a trained expert. The goal of magic was to create an immediate change in the world beyond the text (or spell) itself.[2] This intended change was often positive: healing an afflicted patient, removing a demonic threat, or warding off future harm.

Mesopotamian magical rituals outline the different shapes that magic could take. Magic essentially fell along a spectrum of helpful to harmful, with defensive or protective magic lying at one end; magic that changed the state of the patient, sometimes even harming another in the process, in the middle; and witchcraft occupying the entirely harmful and aggressive end of this spectrum.[3] Although some forms of magic—notably love magic (*rāmu*) and magic intending to influence legal proceedings (*egalkura*, or "entering-the-palace") —occupied the hazy middle ground of causing arguable harm to one person to benefit another, witchcraft (*kišpū*) had only harmful intent. No one gained or benefited from the witch's actions, which added to the chaos of the universe.

The various names of witchcraft highlight the different forms that the witch's malignance could take, as well as the fears inherent in Mesopotamian society. We find examples of "cutting-of-the-throat" magic (*zikurudû*), "seizing-of-the-mouth" magic (*kadabbedû*), "overturning-of-justice" magic (*dibalû*), and hate magic (*zīru*), among others.[4] Some of these may have explained actual physical ailments, with kadabbedû being often linked to speech impediments, such as aphasia. Mesopotamian society had a robust legal system to settle all

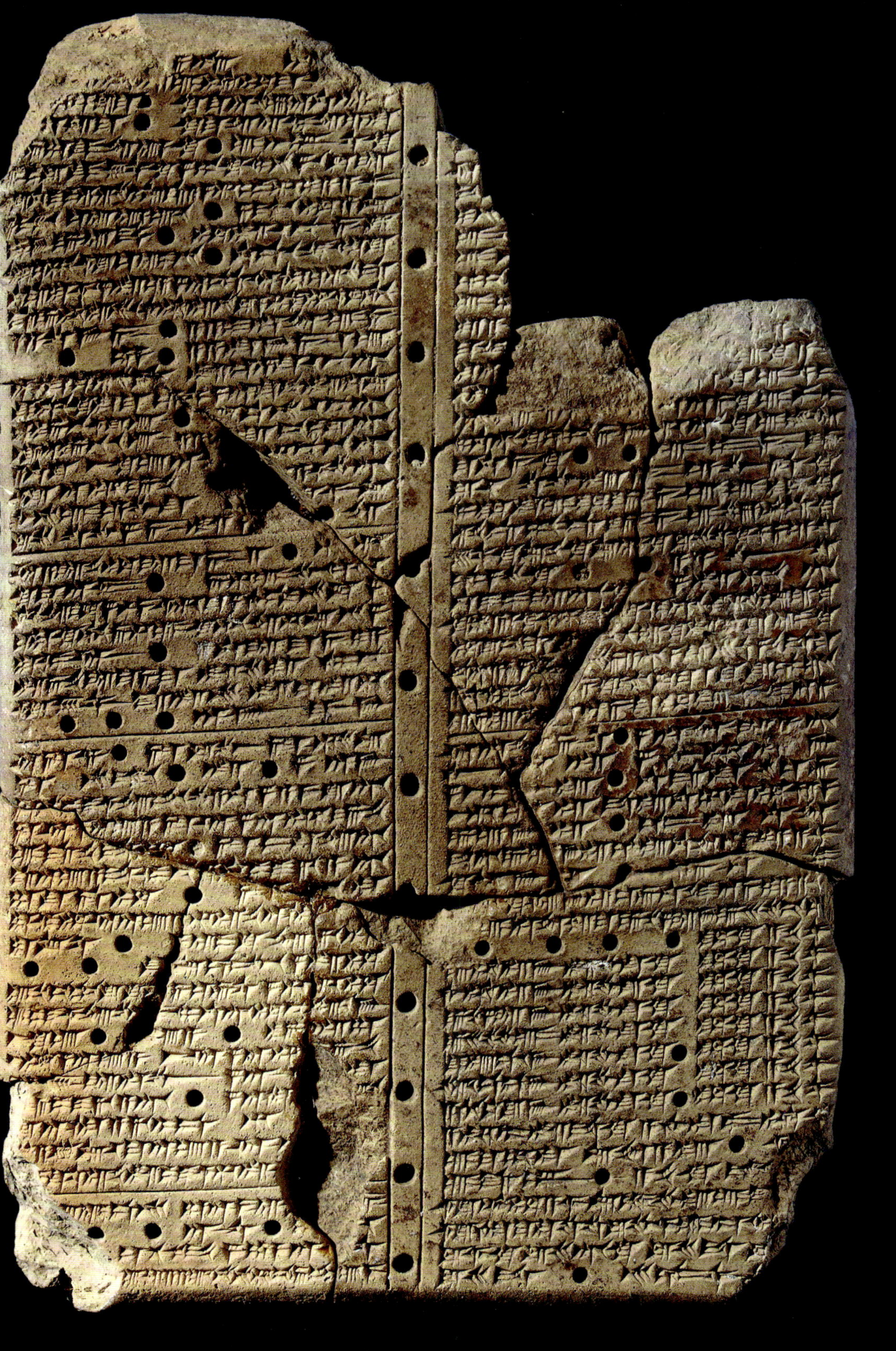

manner of disputes, and the fear of harmful external forces causing one to be disadvantaged or lose a court case may explain the manifestations of witchcraft like kadabbedû and dibalû. Witchcraft could also blur the lines between life and death. The witch might create a figurine of the patient to place in the lap of a corpse, thus binding him to the deceased. Because purely aggressive magic, or *kišpū*, was never recorded in writing, our understanding of the details of witchcraft and its attacks comes from the wide range of anti-witchcraft incantations and rituals that were designed to counter it. These incantations described the witch's attack in specific detail so that its aggression could then be reversed and nullified.[5]

Just like her witchcraft, the witch herself (*kaššāptu*) was a complicated figure, one who occupied different positions in Mesopotamian thought. Though she was usually presented as female, male witches (*kaššāpu*) are also found, often appearing in a pair with the female witch. Fundamentally, the witch existed in two different forms within the Mesopotamian magical tradition. On the one hand, she could be identified with an actual person, a specific individual who could be subsequently targeted and even killed. This version appears in a few recorded legal cases involving witchcraft accusations as well as legal codes recounting the consequences for the same, including the famous Code of Hammurabi. Such accusations were rare in Mesopotamia, however, and the witch as a known individual—or, in other words, an actual person—also appears to have been rare.[6] The witch was far more often represented as something more than human: she was a chaotic force, with abilities and powers similar to the demonic—or the divine. The chaotic, demonic witch exhibited terrifying powers that were fundamentally unsanctioned, even illegitimate.[7] Her actions were counter to the proper order of society, as well as the Mesopotamian world as a whole. This version of the witch could not be countered by mundane means. Instead, she had to be combated by a similarly powerful—though learned and legitimate— ritual figure.

The witch met her equal in the form of the ritual specialist known as the *āšipu*, a term that is often translated as "exorcist." The āšipu was one of a number of trained ritual practitioners in Mesopotamia, a group that also included figures such as the physician (*asû*), the diviner (*bārû*), and others. Though the border between the asû and the āšipu was sometimes hazy, in general the former treated the physical symptoms of an illness, often through pharmacological means, while the latter targeted the demonic or magical cause of the affliction.[8] To aid him in these efforts, the exorcist had a number of tools at his disposal including incantations and rituals, often written and recited; a range of benevolently inclined demonic figures, such as a "good" *udug* or *lamma*; and, most importantly, the legitimation and sanction of particular deities.

Each of these protections was itself complex. Though protective and curative incantations are attested as early as the third millennium BCE, most of the exorcist's textual toolkit dates to the first millennium. One particularly significant text, known as the Exorcist's Manual, outlines a vast corpus of ritual and incantations that the exorcist was, at least in theory, expected to master.[9] The difficult technical nature of the exorcist's craft required a high degree of training and skill, and we see evidence that the profession could be hereditary, with instruction, on some level, being passed down from father to son.[10] The patriarchal nature of Mesopotamian society excluded the vast majority of women from such a profession.

The exorcist's other tools were more decidedly demonic—and divine. He could call upon a wide range of protective figures, many of which also, in other circumstances, demonstrated malevolent behaviour. This shifting nature was common among demons in Mesopotamia, and it was not unusual for the "good" udug demon to stand at the side of the exorcist and help him oppose the "evil" udug actively threatening the patient.[11] The exorcist was also protected by his association with divine figures and the legitimation they provided. In particular, he was connected to the god Enki (also known as Ea), who was linked to wisdom and protective or curative rituals and magic. In some incantations, the exorcist would position himself as a deity presenting the problem afflicting the patient to Enki, to then be given a ritual solution from the deity himself. The entire incantation was thereby imbued with a divine origin and similarly divine legitimation. In other incantations, the exorcist might declare that the very spell was not his own but belonged to the gods. He could also call himself the "exorcist of Eridu," linking himself directly with Enki's patron city and thus reinforcing the legitimation and protection the deity provided.[12]

Both the witch and the exorcist existed within a world that was also populated by a wide range of demonic and monstrous figures, a "Mesopotamian pandemonium."[13] As with the witch, Mesopotamian texts as a whole boasted both a range of individual targeted incantations and other sweeping, extensive series of incantations designed to drive out aggressive, malevolent demons and the threats they

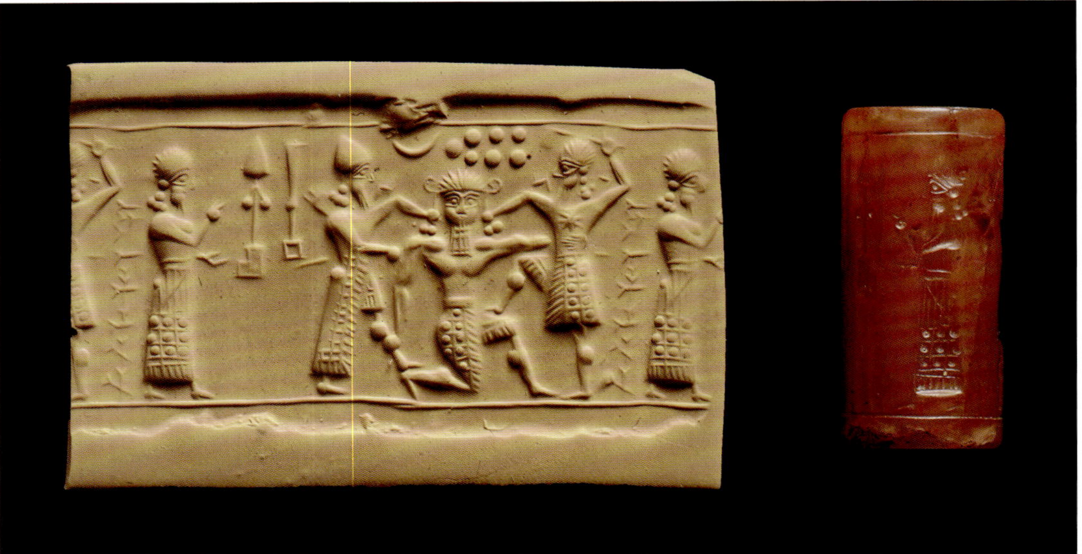

posed.[14] Anything from illness to impotence, from crop failure to simple bad luck, could potentially be attributed to a malevolent demonic cause.

Many demons were described in the abstract and in negation: they were formless, shapeless, and without family or kin. The term *udug* could be used to describe demons as a broad category as well as an individual type of demon. Across this diverse category, demons exhibited some generally shared traits. They were associated with poison and bile, and their gaze could carry its own force. They originated from the Netherworld, moving into the inhabited world of the city to threaten it.

Some of these features were shared with monsters, which were more geographically bounded, often confined to their particular distant locale. The most famous monster originated in the literary space of the Akkadian *Epic of Gilgamesh*, Mesopotamia's best-known literary epic. In a pivotal episode in the text, the titular hero-king ventures to the distant land of the Cedar Forest to claim its bounty of trees and so establish his own renown. In doing so, he must defeat the monstrous Humbaba, the guardian of the Cedar Forest, a figure who is described in terrifying terms as possessing a gaze that is like death. This battle, and Gilgamesh's subsequent victory, remained a popular motif that was often showcased on Mesopotamian cylinder seals (fig. 2). Humbaba escapes his literary origins, in a sense, and

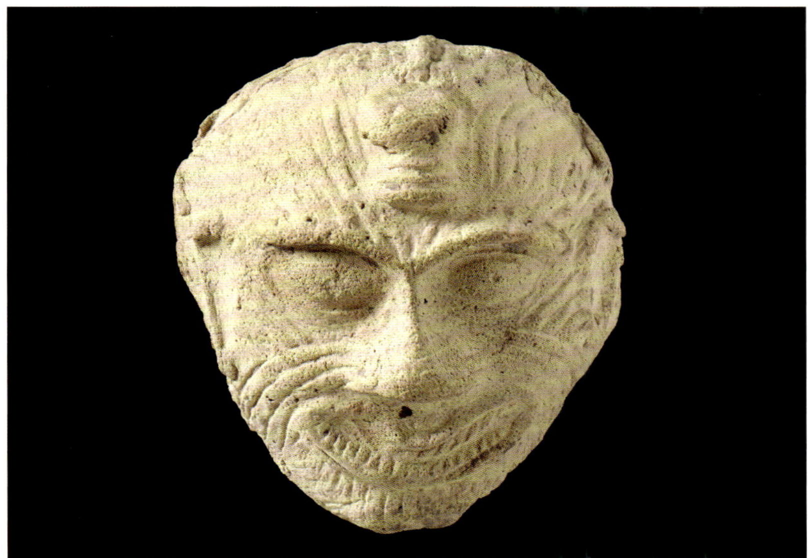

acquires a protective use of his own, with his fierce visage and terrifying gaze providing outward-facing protection wherever he was placed (fig. 3). The qualities that made him such an effective antagonist—his strength, powerful gaze, and other monstrous features—could now be redirected to protective ends.[15]

We find similarly unique profiles in two of Mesopotamia's most well-known demonic figures: the demoness Lamashtu and her counterpart, Pazuzu. Both are outliers among demons, with unique features, well-represented and -defined artistic iconography, and clear origin stories. Lamashtu is a female demon found from the early second millennium BCE onward. Although many demons could have variable natures, Lamashtu was only ever malevolent, with a very particular and rather grisly purpose. As described in the long ritual series that counters her, she was originally divine but was cast out from the heavens because of her penchant for targeting infants and pregnant women in particular.[16] Once denied worship as a deity, she became altogether malevolent and represented a major threat to the young, undoubtedly representing the dangers of pregnancy, childbirth, and high rates of infant mortality seen in Mesopotamia. The rituals to counter her describe her behavior in detail. She follows after pregnant women, and "those about to give birth she puts under a spell: 'Bring me your sons—I want to suckle (them)! In the mouth of your daughters I want to place (my) breast.' She holds in her hand

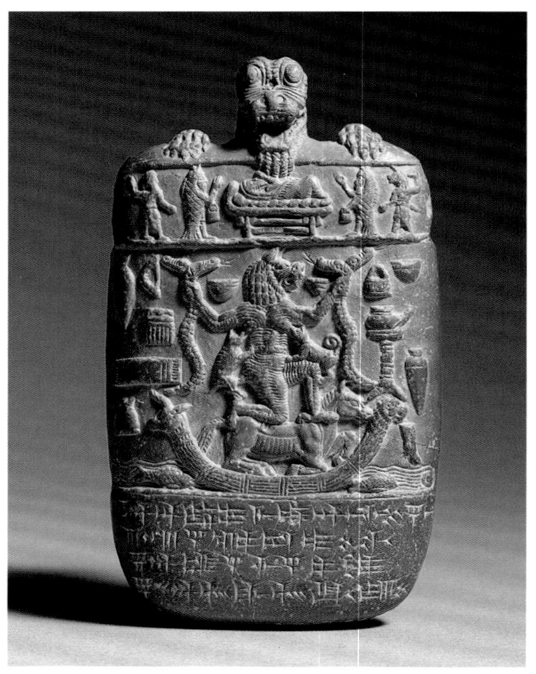
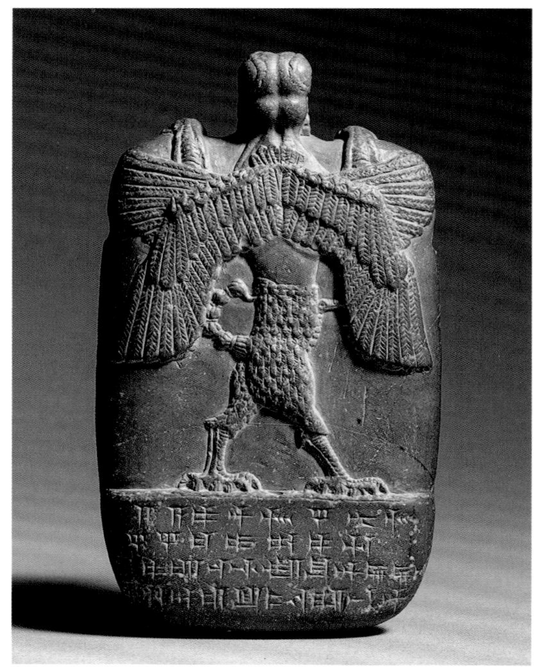

fever, cold, chills, frost."[17] Lamashtu's actions are also represented in her iconography, found in amulets designed to counter her (see fig. 7). She is depicted with a lion's snarling face, grasping snakes in her many-taloned hands, while a piglet and puppy suckle at her breasts (fig. 4). In many ways, Lamashtu reflects an inversion of motherhood: instead of cradling an infant, her hands might strangle them, and the milk she offers is poison, fit only for beasts.

In the first millennium, a new opponent to Lamashtu appeared: the demon Pazuzu. Pazuzu was characterized by a distinctive masculinity that served to counter Lamashtu's traits. Pazuzu was also a mix of creatures, with clawed hands and taloned feet, a snarling leonine head, and four outstretched wings (fig. 5). When displayed in his full form, he is an odd mix of frailty—with prominent, nearly emaciated ribs—and strength, even virility, given his erect, snake-headed penis. His terrifying visage warded off Lamashtu, and images of him were intended to be worn to guard against her, whether that image was of his full form or reduced to his head and gaze alone (fig. 6). Among the various rituals that drive out Lamashtu, one describes drawing the demoness out of the patient through the use of her figurine, giving that figurine food, provisions, and offerings, and setting all this

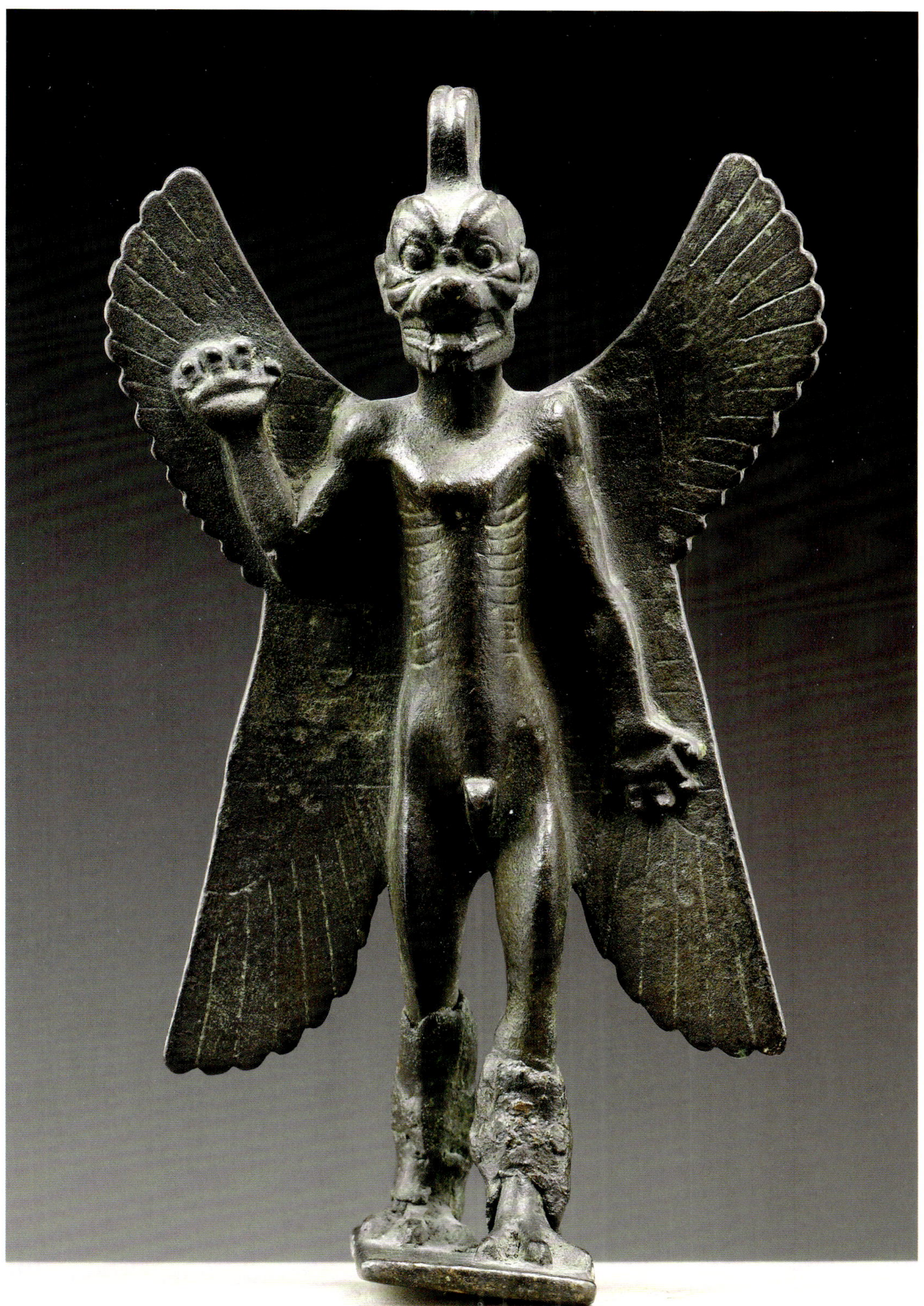

FIG. 6
Amulet with the demon
Pazuzu, 681–627 BCE

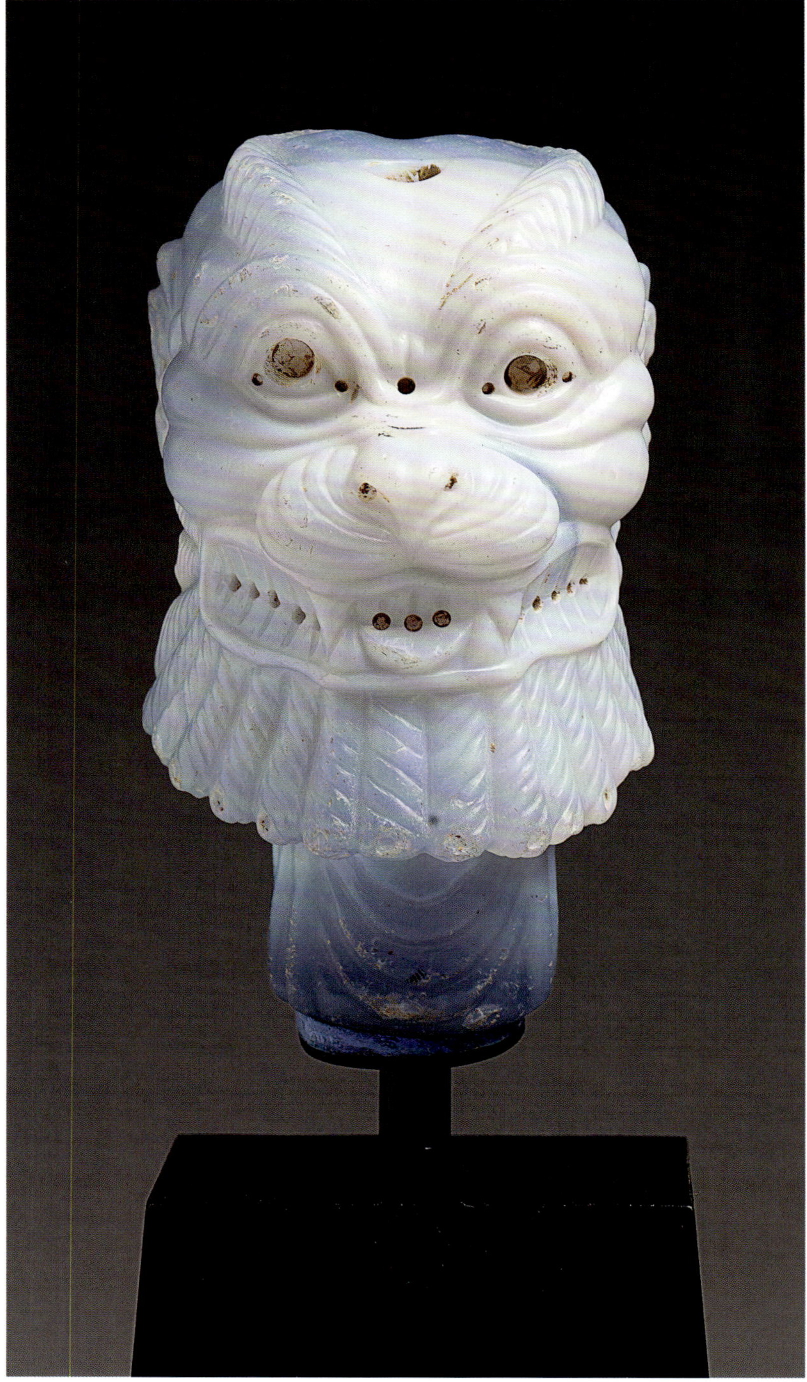

outside the city wall. In this way, Lamashtu
will be cast away from the city, forced to cross
the steppe and eventually journey into the
Netherworld once again. This narrative is
inscribed on the amulets that counter her,
often with the incorporation of Pazuzu to
help force the demoness along (fig. 4).

Pazuzu highlights a final important point
about Mesopotamian magic. Many of these
figures were capable of either helping or hurt-
ing, of doing good or causing harm. Whether
a demon would act benevolently or malevo-
lently might often be determined by where it
appeared within the narrative of the incantation itself. When establishing the threat, an
antagonist was required, while combating
it in the hopes of a cure necessitated a beneficial agent. In this manner, the "evil udug"
could be opposed by the "good udug" within
the space of a single text. Moreover, with a
few exceptions, the lines between demon
and deity are similarly ill-defined. For example, Pazuzu was utilized
to positive purposes, but he was not inherently beneficial as much as
he was directable. Pazuzu intends to combat Lamashtu, and an
afflicted individual may benefit from that battle, but such positive
outcomes are ancillary to Pazuzu. In the end, his own ferocity has
merely been guided in a helpful direction but remains, to a degree,
uncontrolled. Similarly, both the Mesopotamian exorcist and the
witch demonstrated comparable inherent powers and possible
abilities, to the point they even occupied similar categories: somewhat more than human, but nevertheless capable of interacting with
the inhabited world. They differed, of course, in their intent, and thus
their effect—and, most importantly, in whether the power they
wielded was seen as legitimate and justified or unsanctioned and
thus dangerous.

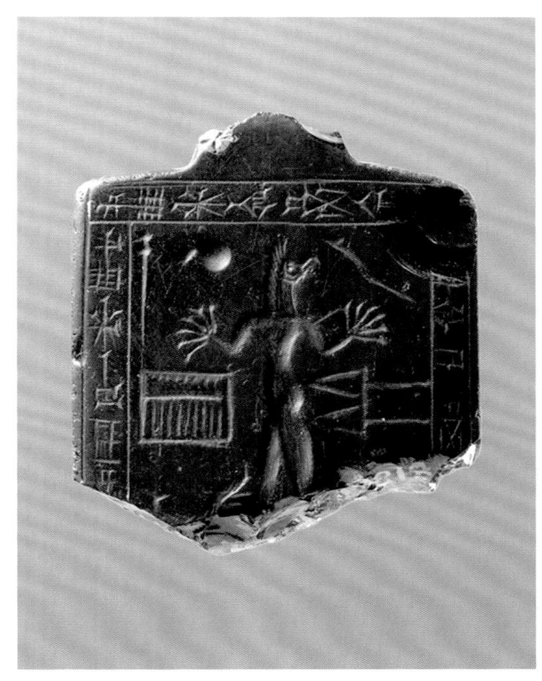

1. *Maqlû* 7: 55–56, 69; see Tzvi Abusch, *The Magical Ceremony Maqlû: A Critical Edition* (Brill, 2016), 352–53. The full text of the Maqlû has been edited most recently in that volume, with further discussion on the text and its transmission history in Daniel Schwemer, *The Anti-Witchcraft Ritual Maqlû: The Cuneiform Sources of a Magic Ceremony from Ancient Mesopotamia* (Harrassowitz Verlag, 2017).

2. Daniel Schwemer, "Magic Rituals: Conceptualization and Performance," in *The Cambridge History of Magic and Witchcraft in the West: From Antiquity to the Present*, ed. David J. Collins (Cambridge University Press, 2018), 19.

3. Schwemer, "Magic Rituals," 26–34.

4. Daniel Schwemer, "Cultural Constructions of Ambiguous, Unsanctioned, or Illegitimate Ritual: Mesopotamia," in *Guide to the Study of Ancient Magic*, ed. David Frankfurter (Brill, 2019), 42–43.

5. The range of Mesopotamian anti-witchcraft incantations has been collected and published by a team at the University of Würzburg and can be found online (see https://oracc.museum.upenn.edu/cmawro) as well as in three published volumes; the first of these includes an overview of the nature of anti-witchcraft rituals as a whole. See Tzvi Abusch and Daniel Schwemer, *Corpus of Mesopotamian Anti-Witchcraft Rituals*, vol. 1 (Brill, 2011), 1–25.

6. One of the few recorded examples of a witchcraft accusation is found in an Old Babylonian (around 1800 BCE) group of letters. The five tablets describe a case presented against Ur-Šubula and his wife and mother-in-law by his father, Ili-iddinam. While the initial dispute was over payment of a share of crops, Ili-iddinam insisted that the situation was influenced by witchcraft and charged Ur-Šubula's wife and mother-in-law (though not Ur-Šubula himself) as witches and brought the affair to court in order to stop their activity; see Stanley D. Walters, "The Sorceress and Her Apprentice: A Case Study of an Accusation," *Journal of Cuneiform Studies* 23, no. 2 (1970): 27–38.

7. On the dual nature of the witch in Mesopotamia, see Tzvi Abusch, "The Demonic Image of the Witch in Standard Babylonian Literature: The Reworking of Popular Conceptions by Learned Exorcists," in *Religion, Science, and Magic: In Concert and in Conflict*, ed. Jacob Neuzner, Ernest S. Frerichs, and Paul Virgil McCracken Flesher (Oxford University Press, 1989), 27–58 and Gina Konstantopoulos, "Demons and Exorcism in Mesopotamia," *Religion Compass* 14 (2020): 6–8.

8. Konstantopoulos, "Demons and Exorcism in Mesopotamia," 8.

9. See a recent edition in Markham J. Geller, "The Exorcist's Manual (KAR 44)," in *Assyrian and Babylonian Scholarly Text Catalogues: Medicine, Magic, and Divination*, ed. Ulrike Steinert (De Gruyter Brill 2020), 292–312. The Exorcist's Manual likely represented an idealized version of the sum total of the knowledge of the exorcist's craft, as well as reinforcing the need for divine legitimation and support, as the range of texts was so vast that no single person could hope to master all of them.

10. Natalie Naomi May, "Exorcists and Physicians at Assur: More on Their Education and Interfamily and Court Connections," *Zeitschrift für Assyriologie* 108, no. 1 (2018): 63–80.

11. On the nature of these figures in Mesopotamia, see the overview in Gina Konstantopoulos, *The Divine/Demonic Seven and the Place of Demons in Mesopotamia* (Brill, 2023), 30–50.

12. Konstantopoulos, "Demons and Exorcism in Mesopotamia," 9; Nils P. Heeßel, "'I Am the Messenger of the Great Gods': Some Thoughts on a Legitimising Statement," in *Legitimising Magic: Strategies and Practices in Ancient Mesopotamia,* ed. Nils P. Heeßel and Elyze Zomer (Brill, 2024), 5–15.

13. Frans A. M. Wiggermann, "The Mesopotamian Pandemonium: A Provisional Census," in *Demoni mesopotamici,* ed. D. O. Edzard and M. P. Streck (Sapienza University, 2011), 298–322.

14. The most notable of such was undoubtedly the incantation series entitled *Udug Hul,* literally "Evil Demons"; see the edition in Markham J. Geller, *Healing Magic and Evil Demons: Canonical Udug-hul Incantations* (Walter de Gruyter, 2016).

15. Sarah Graff, "The Head of Humbaba," *Archiv für Religionsgeschichte* 14, no. 1 (2013): 129–42.

16. Walter Farber, *Lamaštu: An Edition of the Canonical Series of Lamaštu Incantations and Rituals and Related Texts from the Second and First Millennia B.C.* (Eisenbrauns, 2014).

17. Farber, *Lamaštu,* 155, lines 120–23.

Magic in Classical Greece

JEFFREY SPIER

IN CLASSICAL GREECE, unlike Egypt and Mesopotamia, magical practices were only very rarely associated with conventional religion. They were typically believed to be something that foreigners brought to Greece and were regarded with suspicion and scorn. Only the Greek *mantis* (seer), a hereditary and sometimes itinerant priest who acted as interpreter of omens sent by the gods, might be considered an individual with legitimate magical powers. Nevertheless, there was a widespread belief in the supernatural, including monsters; the influence of the dead on the living; and the power of plants, stones, and other natural materials to cure medical ailments and to protect from harm. Greeks learned to make use of these powers, even if they were sometimes viewed warily.

In Homer's *Odyssey* (which dates to around 700 BCE), the hero Odysseus encounters a number of daunting supernatural situations on his journey to return home after the Trojan War. Aside from a variety of monstrous creatures, he and his men must confront the divine sorceress Circe, who, with a special potion and magic wand, transforms all the luckless sailors who land on her remote island into wild beasts (figs. 1, 2). As wolves, lions, and boars they roam her house, fawning at her feet. After some of his companions are turned into animals, Odysseus is saved by the god Hermes, who gives the hero a magic herb that protects him from Circe's powers, allowing him to force her to return his men to human form. The elements of this story may seem more like those of a folktale than actual magic practices, but the use of rare plants to cure or enchant is widely attested in the ancient world. More significantly, the persona of the powerful foreign sorceress, whom Circe exemplifies, is a recurring feature in Greek belief.

Calyx-krater with
Odysseus and Circe,
about 440 BCE

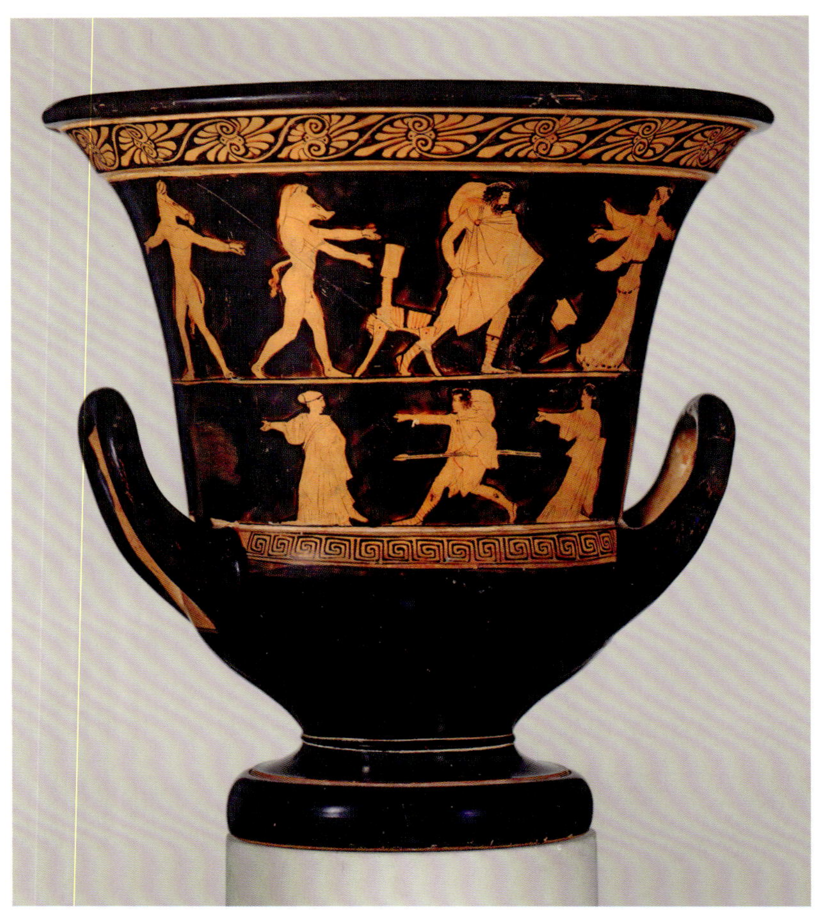

Kylix with scenes from
the *Odyssey*, 550–525 BCE

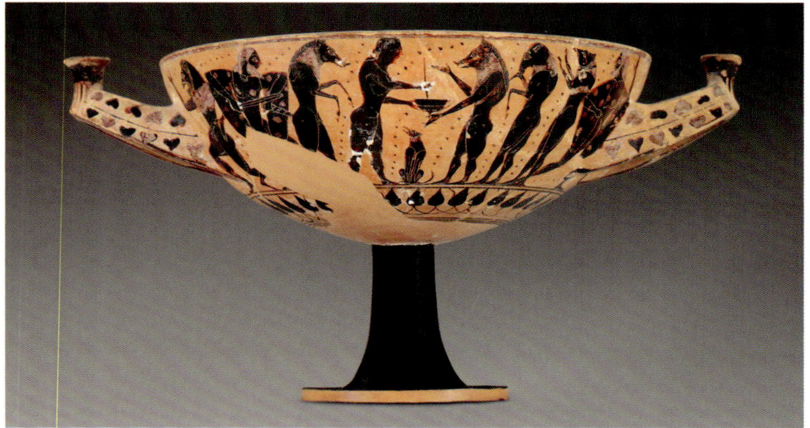

Medea, Circe's niece by some accounts, has an even greater presence in Greek myth. Although not mentioned by Homer, she is named by Hesiod (around 700 BCE) and is the subject of numerous poems and plays, including those of the Athenian playwrights Sophocles (though these works are unfortunately lost) and Euripides. She lived in far-off Colchis, on the east coast of the Black Sea, where she met the Greek hero Jason and his companions, the Argonauts, who were in search of the Golden Fleece. Falling in love with the hero, she assists him in taking the fleece, abandons her home while allowing her brother to be murdered, and provides Jason with various magical ointments and potions (fig. 3). She assists him in claiming the throne of Iolcus, in northern Greece, from King Pelias through a combination of magic and deceit: She demonstrates her ability to rejuvenate an old ram by cutting it into pieces and placing them into a boiling potion (fig. 4). When the king's daughters attempt to replicate the procedure with Pelias, he, instead, perishes.

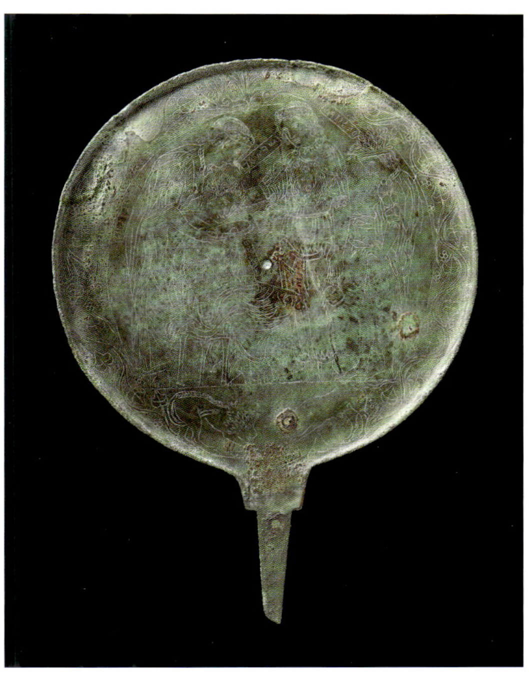

FIG. 3
Mirror with Medea offering a potion to Jason, about 400 BCE

In some versions of the Jason and Medea myth, it is the goddess Aphrodite who—as the mid-fifth-century BCE poet Pindar states—"taught Jason to be skillful in prayers and charms, in order that he might strip Medea of reverence for her parents, and that desire for Greece might shake her with the whip of Persuasion as she was burning in her heart."[1] The magical implement the goddess used as a love charm was the *iunx*, originally a bird pinned to a wheel but later merely a spinning wheel on a cord, like a child's toy, which is sometimes seen in the hands of Eros (fig. 5). Also having magical aspects are the women skilled in the use of plants for healing, such as the Elean princess Agadame, who is mentioned fleetingly in the *Iliad* as one "who knew all the medicines grown in the earth."[2] Thessaly, in northern Greece, was considered the home for such practices, and the Thessalian sorceress became a familiar character in Greek literature.

Although the foreignness of magic is often stressed in Greek myth, Greek men and women also could be adept in such practices. Another story in the *Odyssey* relates that Odysseus, having been

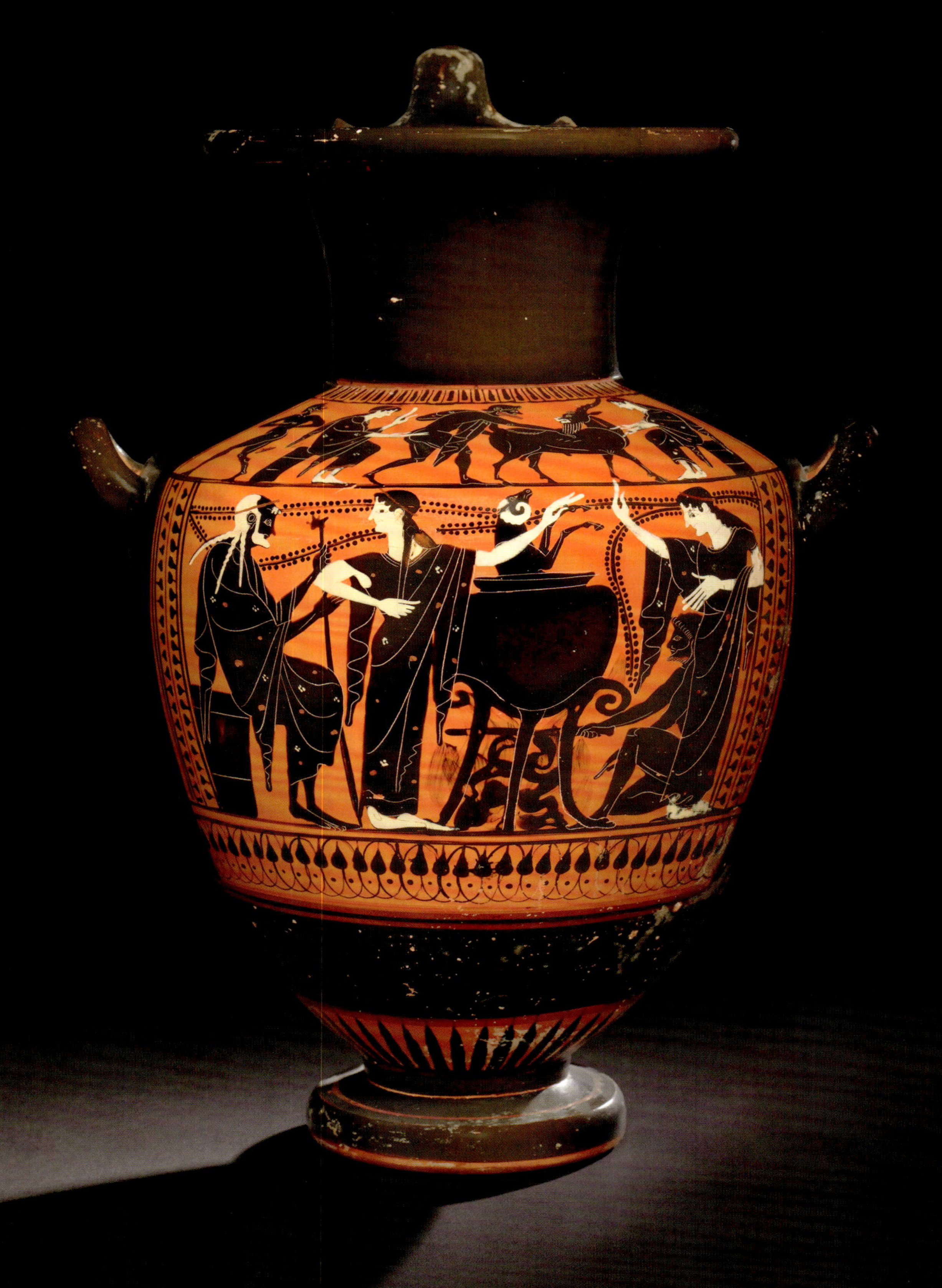

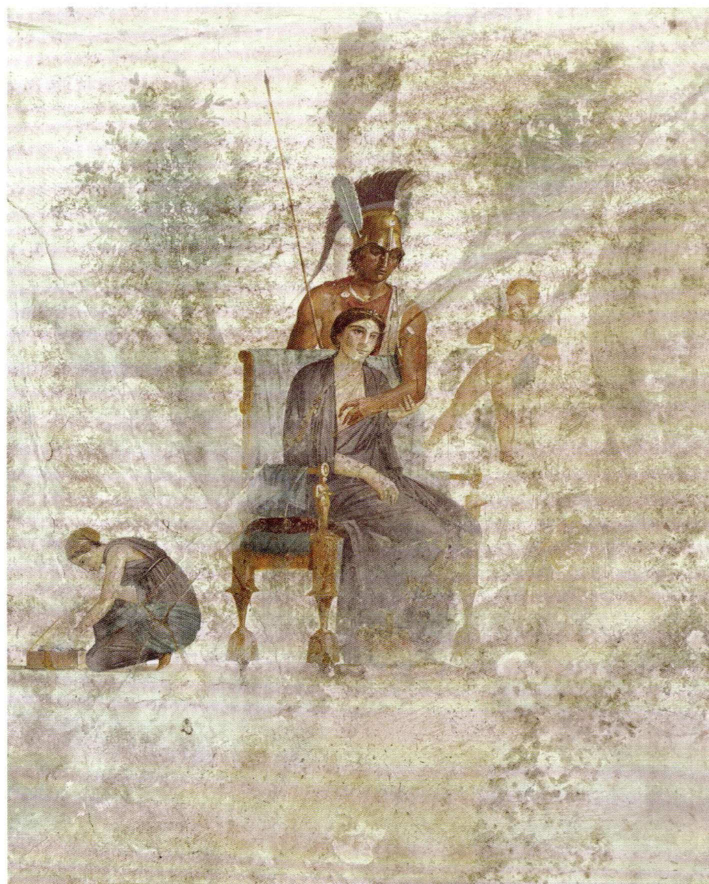

wounded by a wild boar while hunting, was healed by his companions, the sons of Autolycus, who "tended to him and skillfully bound up the wound [...] and with an incantation they stopped the dark blood."[3] Reciting a charm to aid healing appears to have been common practice, and a variety of poetic verses served to cure fever, migraine, and other ailments.

Many later classical texts describe women who were skilled at healing with potions and purveyors of love charms, and these stories no doubt reflect actual practices. Love charms, in particular, figure prominently in actual Greek magical practice. Deities of the Underworld and ghosts were typically invoked to coerce the desired parties for erotic aims. The third-century BCE Sicilian writer Theocritus composed a memorable picture of such a woman in his Idyll 2 (sometimes called "The Sorceress"), in which Smithaea, a woman on the island of Cos, casts a love charm that includes an invocation of the magical iunx wheel, the burning of herbs, the melting of a wax effigy, and the recitation of a long poetic text to bring her lover, Delphis, back to her. She calls to her servant, Thestylis:

> Where are my laurel leaves? Bring them, Thestylis. Where are my love-charms? Wreathe the bowl with crimson wool, so I may bind my cruel lover who brings me pain, who, wretched me, hasn't even come to my door for twelve days, nor knows whether I am dead or alive. The heartless one hasn't even knocked. Surely both swift-minded Eros and Aphrodite have led him elsewhere. Tomorrow I'll go to Timagetus'[s] wrestling school to see him, and I'll reproach him for how he treats me. But now I'll bind him with sacrifices. So, Moon, shine bright, for to you I'll softly chant, goddess, and to chthonian Hecate, whom even dogs tremble at as she comes through corpses and black blood. Hail, dread Hecate, and stay with us until the end, making these potions no weaker than those of Circe or Medea or golden-haired Perimede. Iunx, draw that man to my house.[4]

These women also made small charms, often with knotted threads, that were worn for protection. The Athenian statesman Pericles, as he lay dying of plague in 429 BCE, "being visited by one of his friends, showed him an amulet that the women had hung around his neck, indicating how extremely ill he must be to submit to such foolishness."[5] This anecdote demonstrates that although educated Athenians might treat such amulets with derision, they were used nonetheless.

Only somewhat more respected, if we are to believe the moralizing Greek authors, were the itinerant priests and seers who offered their services for a fee. Plato, who regarded such activities as impious, wrote around the mid-fourth century BCE:

> Begging priests and seers go to the doors of the wealthy and persuade them that they possess a god-given power to heal with sacrifices and incantations any wrong deed committed by the person themselves

or their ancestors, with pleasurable feasts. And if someone wishes to harm an enemy, they will, for a small fee, harm either a just or unjust person alike with certain magical rites and binding spells, claiming to persuade the gods to serve them [...] And they produce a jumble of books by Musaeus and Orpheus, offspring, they say, of the Moon and the Muses, according to which they perform their rituals, persuading not only private individuals but even entire cities that there exist, both for the living and for the dead, absolutions and purifications from wrongdoings through sacrifices and pleasant games—which they call mysteries —that free us from the evils of the afterlife, while terrible things await those who do not perform the sacrifices.[6]

The belief in spirits of the dead and their influence on the living was widespread in the ancient world, including Greece. An early example again comes from Homer. Following his departure from Circe's island, Odysseus must travel to the Underworld to consult the ghost of the seer Teiresias in order to learn how to return home to Ithaca. Necromancy, the notion that specific knowledge could be gained by consulting the dead, was shared by various Mediterranean cultures and survived well into Roman times. On his arrival in the Underworld, Odysseus must sacrifice two rams, for the blood attracts the souls of the dead. First, he meets the ghost of his helmsman, Elpenor, who died accidentally and pleads for proper burial (fig. 6). Odysseus is then able to speak with Teiresias, as well as other departed acquaintances. This uncanny episode has folkloric characteristics, but it also preserves common magical beliefs about the powers of the dead.

It is certain that many magical beliefs were introduced to Greece from Egypt and the Near East by the seventh century BCE if not before, although how this process occurred is not entirely clear. No doubt, Greek merchants returning from these regions would have brought tales of the supernatural and even foreign rituals. The encounters with wondrous beings in the *Odyssey* reflect such origins, and there are other indications as well, such as the late-seventh-century BCE poet Sappho's reference to the "child-loving Gello," a Babylonian demon (like Lamashtu) who preyed on children.[7] The many Greeks living on the coast of western Asia Minor may well have

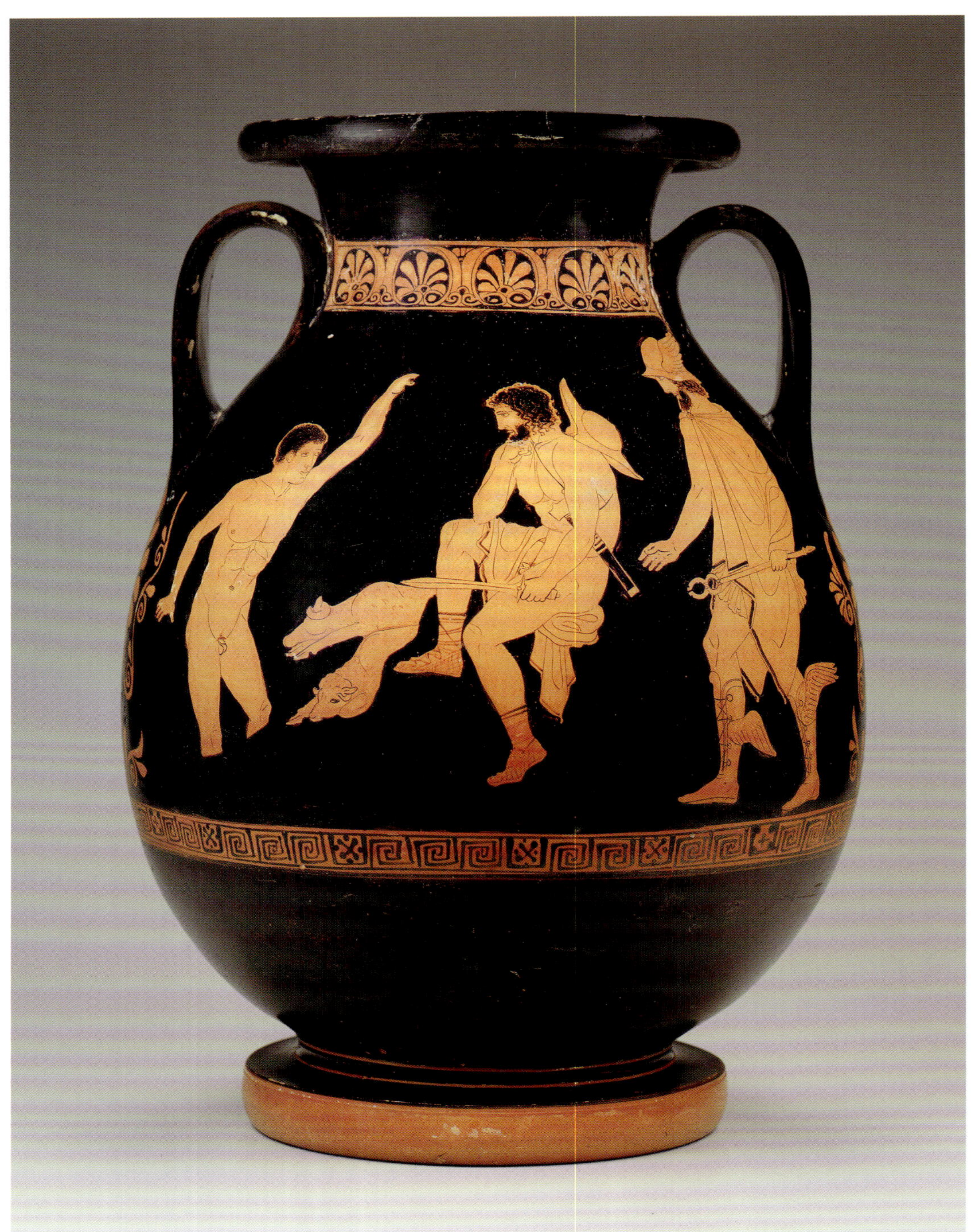

encountered the Persian hereditary priests known as the Magi, who accompanied King Xerxes in his campaign against Greece in 480 BCE and performed unusual, even shocking, rituals including human sacrifice, which were noted by the fifth-century BCE Greek historians.[8] There is even some evidence for Persian and Babylonian priests visiting Athens in the late fifth century BCE.[9]

Archaeological evidence for magical practices is confined largely to materials that can survive burial, for the most part inscribed tablets and figures made of lead. These practices find parallels in earlier Egyptian, Assyrian, and Hittite rituals. For example, when Greeks from the island of Thera set off to establish the new city of Cyrene on the coast of Libya in the seventh century BCE, they participated in a magical ritual, burning wax effigies and swearing an oath: "May he, who does not abide by this agreement but transgresses it, melt away and dissolve like the images."[10] Other civic rituals intended to protect the community from harm (such as plague) took the form of poetic recitations that were then inscribed on lead tablets.

Small effigies also served as love charms and curses. Several lead figurines, sometimes depicted with hands bound and placed in coffin-like boxes, have been discovered in Athens and elsewhere in Greece, dating mostly from the fourth century BCE or later (fig. 7). Those with inscriptions on them suggest they cursed rivals in legal disputes. First attested in the Greek cities in Sicily around 500 BCE, curse tablets

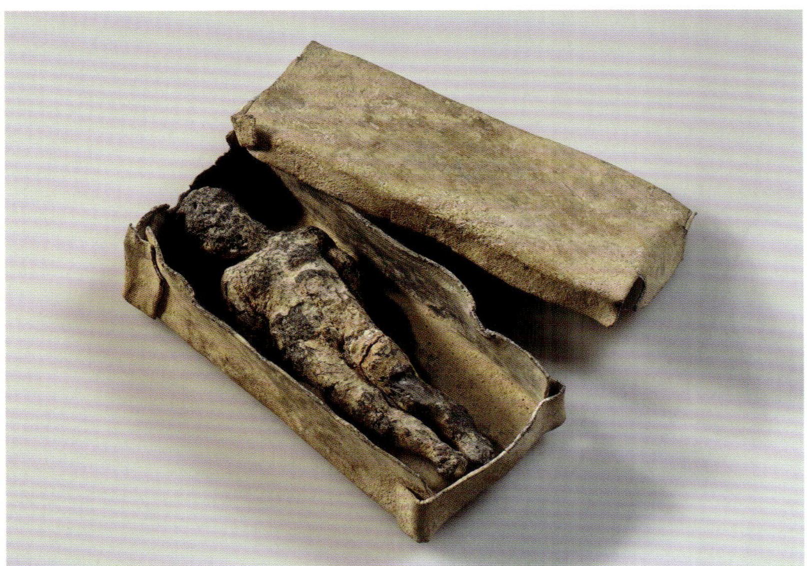

FIG. 7
Miniature coffin with curse figure, 4th century BCE

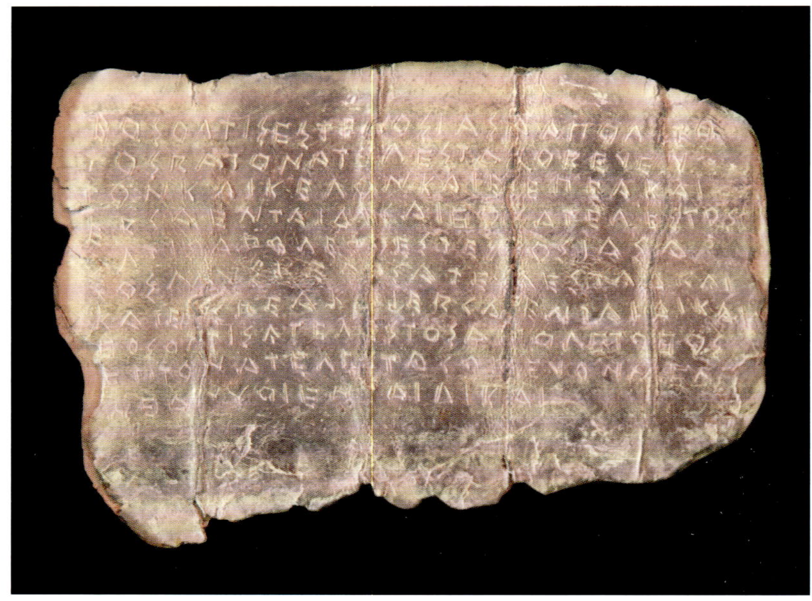

soon proliferated in the Greek-speaking world and continued to be made well into the Roman period (fig. 8). They typically invoked the deities of the Underworld—Hekate, Hades, Persephone, and "chthonic" Artemis and Hermes—who are asked to do the aggrieved individual's bidding and "bind" the named adversaries. Love charms, too, made use of similar aggressive, even violent, imagery in invoking deities and spirits of the dead.

It is uncertain who wrote these charms and curses, but it seems that self-identifying seers or other specialists in magic set up their practices in the marketplaces of cities throughout the Greek world. They were stocked with lead tablets and ready to write out texts tailored to specific clients, who then deposited the objects in graves, wells, or other places thought to have connections to the Underworld.

Despite the dismissal of the practitioners of magic as foolish, greedy, and immoral by the educated classes of Greece, magic flour-ished in everyday life, with many turning to the use of protective amulets, love charms, and curses in times of uncertainty. The tension between rational and magical belief is especially evident in the writings of Plato, who disparages the activities of the magicians and their patrons. It is likely that the belief in magic in classical Greece was far more widespread than the literary sources and the archaeo-logical record report.

NOTES

1. Pindar, *Pythian* 4.213–19.

2. *Iliad* 11.739.

3. *Odyssey* 10.209–574.

4. A. S. F. Gow, ed., *Theocritus*, vol. 1 (Cambridge University Press, 1952), 16–17.

5. Plutarch, *Pericles* 38.

6. Plato, *Republic* 364b–365a.

7. Edgar Lobel and Denys Page, eds., *Poetarum Lesbiorum Fragmenta* (Clarendon Press, 1963), 101, fragment 178.

8. In *The Histories* 7.113–14, Herodotus describes the sacrifice of white horses at the River Strymon and of young boys and girls of the Edonian tribe buried alive in Thrace.

9. See Peter Kingsley, "Meetings with Magi: Iranian Themes Among the Greeks, from Xanthus of Lydia to Plato's Academy," *Journal of the Royal Asiatic Society* 5, no. 2 (1995): 173–209.

10. Christopher A. Faraone, "Molten Wax, Spilt Wine and Mutilated Animals: Sympathetic Magic in Near Eastern and Early Greek Oath Ceremonies," *Journal of Hellenic Studies* 113 (1993): 60–61.

Magic in the
Roman Empire

JEFFREY SPIER

BY THE TIME of the establishment of the Roman Empire in the
eastern Mediterranean at the end of the first century BCE, new forms
of magic had emerged that combined many of the centuries-old
magical beliefs of Egypt, Mesopotamia, and Greece with new magical
names, spells, and rituals. Alexander the Great's conquest of Asia
Minor, the Near East, and Egypt between 336 and 323 BCE had led to
a considerable mixing of cultures and the sharing of their varied
traditions. In Mesopotamia, the ancient records of Babylonia—rich in
mathematical, astronomical, and medical information as well as
magical texts—became accessible to Greek scholars. In Egypt, the
priests, who had previously closely guarded their magical knowledge,
found themselves in need of new Greek and Roman clients as
Egyptian temples lost their power and authority under foreign rule.

Although innovations in magical practices no doubt took place
in various cities in the Roman Empire, the great metropolis of
Alexandria in Egypt was likely the most important center. Founded
by Alexander the Great, the vast city was composed not only of
Greek settlers but Egyptians, Babylonians, Jews, Persians, and
others. By the early first century BCE (if not earlier), magical texts
were being composed there in Greek, the common language of the
eastern Mediterranean, incorporating a great variety of spells, magic
words, and instructions for magical procedures drawn from this rich
mix of cultures.

Evidence for these magical practices survives in a variety of
sources. Perhaps most remarkable are actual books of magic spells
and rituals, some written on long papyrus rolls and others in codex
form, all fortunately preserved thanks to the arid sands of Egypt,

which prevented their decay. Over a hundred magical papyri are known, some of which are of substantial length. The earliest examples date to the second century BCE, although the majority are considerably later, belonging to the second to fifth centuries CE. Some are written in Greek, while others are in Egyptian Demotic or the later version of Egyptian known as Coptic. Sometimes the text was written in a code that replaced the Greek letters with symbols, evidently for secrecy (fig. 1). Bilingual books demonstrate that the Egyptian priests were not only studying their own ancient texts but reading Greek works on magic as well.

At least ten of the most significant magical papyri are believed to have been found together in the vicinity of Thebes in Egypt in the early 1800s—a library of sorts, although the identity of the owner (a group of priests? a sophisticated magician? a scholar?) remains unknown.[1] The papyri include handbooks, like recipe books, containing spells for a variety of purposes. Topics range from achieving divine revelation to more mundane matters, such as winning at dice or keeping bugs out of the house. The spells promise foreknowledge, ways to summon demonic assistants, protection from evil forces, and cures for scorpion stings and a variety of other medical ailments. There are also many love charms to attract reluctant mates and curses to harm adversaries in love or business. Some papyri appear to have served as practical guides for professional magicians.

Characteristic of the newer magical practices is the use of elaborate spells that were intended to be both written and recited while performing carefully specified ritual activities. Often the practitioner is instructed to abstain from certain foods, to wear linen robes, and to crown himself with an olive wreath. He may be told to sacrifice a rooster or drown a cat. Special plants might be called for, mixed with honey or unusual substances. Spells may be written with myrrh ink, red cinnabar, or animal blood on papyrus, or on a linen cloth, a laurel leaf, a seashell, or the wing of a bat. Any number of imaginative procedures appear in the magical instructions found in the papyri.

Especially notable are the many magical words prescribed, most of which appear to have been newly introduced in the first century BCE. Many names are of Egyptian derivation, while others are Greek, Babylonian, Persian, or Hebrew. The Jewish names for God— Iao (the Greek transliteration of Yahweh), Sabaoth ("lord of hosts"), and Adonai ("my lord")—as well as the archangels Michael, Gabriel, Raphael, and Ouriel often appear. The name Abrasax is particularly

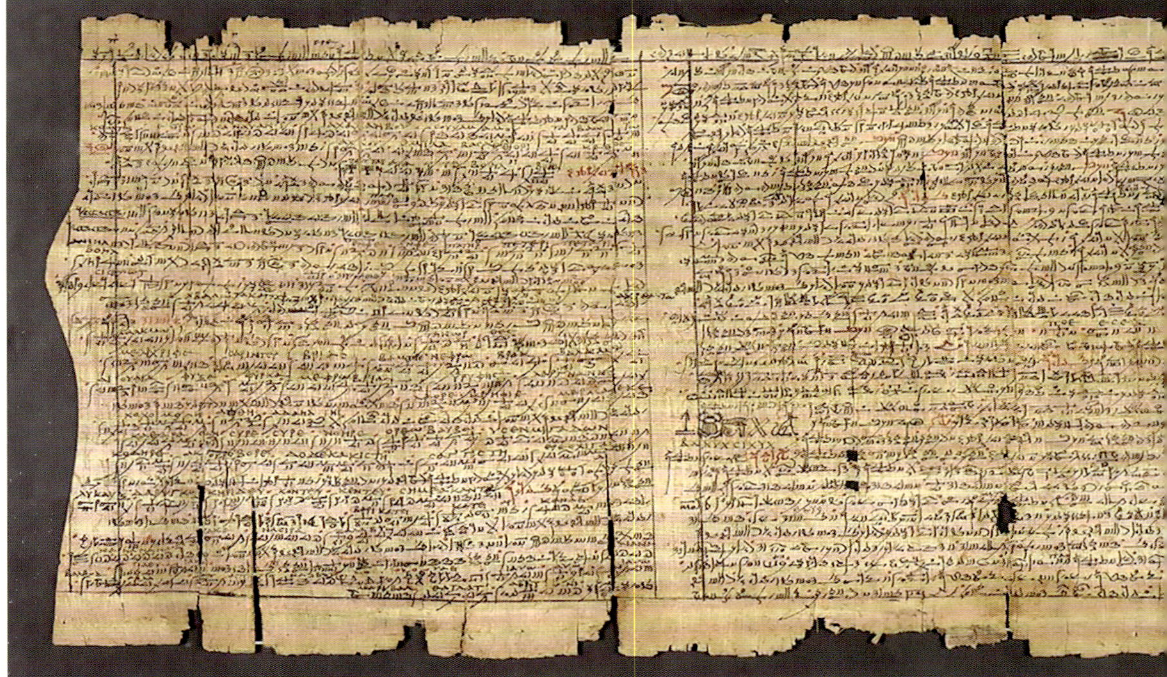

popular in the magical papyri and on amulets, and although its derivation is uncertain, the numerical value of its Greek letters adds up to 365, the number of days of the year, a likely reference to the sun god. The origins of many other names, however, remain entirely unknown. Vowels and palindromes, which were assigned special powers, often occur as well.

A typical string of magical names and vowels occurs in a spell for divine revelation addressed to the sun god, found in a bilingual Greek and Demotic papyrus of the third century CE. The text combines Greek, Egyptian, and Jewish elements, as well as names that are frequently encountered on amulets but are of uncertain derivation (fig. 2):

> I call upon you who are seated in impenetrable dark-
> ness and are in the midst of the great gods; you who,
> when you set, take with you the solar rays and send
> up the light-bringing goddess NEBOUTOSOUALÊTH;
> great god BARZAN BOUBARZAN NARZAZOUZAN
> BARZABOUZATH Helios.

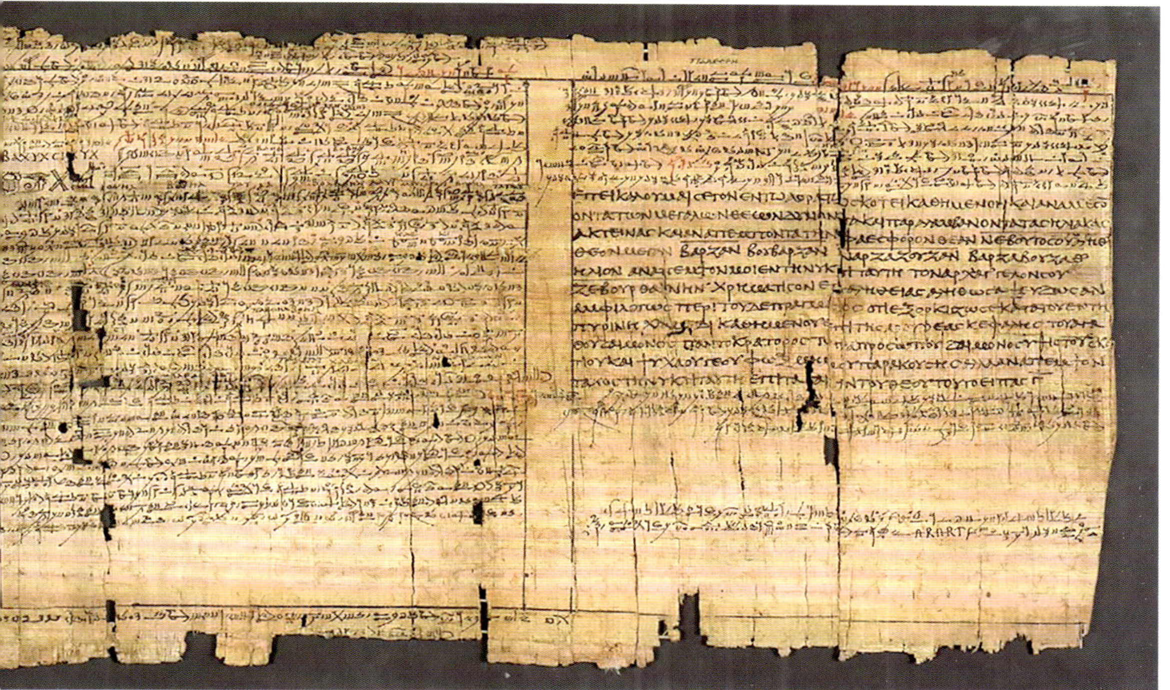

Send up to me in this night your archangel ZEB-
OURTHAUNÊN, respond with truth, truly, not
falsely, unambiguously concerning such-and-such a
matter, because I conjure you by him who is seated
in the fiery cloak on the serpentine head of the
Agathos Daimon, the almighty, four-faced, highest
demon, dark and conjuring, PHÔX. Do not ignore
me, but send up [a revelation] quickly tonight in
accordance with the command of the god. (Say this
three times.) [2]

The magical handbooks written on papyri provide the most
comprehensive example of magical practices in the early Roman
Imperial period, but a large number of actual amulets in various
materials also survive. Some amulets were written by the magician
on scraps of papyrus for their clients, who then folded the amulet
and carried it for protection. One such example, written for a woman
suffering from fever, invokes unnamed gods with a series of magical
words followed by permutations of vowels (fig. 3):

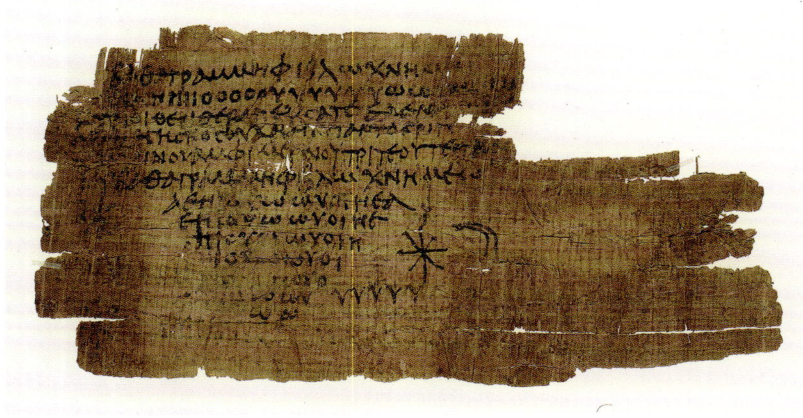

Lord gods, heal Helene, whom [NN] bore, from all illness and from all shivering and fever that which occurs by day, quotidian, tertian, quartan. *Iarbath agramme phiblo chnemeo* (followed by vowels arranged in a triangular pattern).[3]

As in earlier Greek practice, lead curse tablets continued to be used and have been found throughout the Roman Empire. In western Europe (notably England) examples were inscribed in Latin with appeals to the local deity for assistance and do not make use of magical names or words. Elsewhere, however, including at Rome and Carthage, curse tablets and figurines preserve spells similar to those found in the Egyptian papyri, showing how far the Greek-Egyptian magical practices could travel. Lead tablets could also be employed as coercive love charms, invoking the same Underworld deities and spirits of the dead as curses (figs. 4, 5). Erotic attraction was regarded as a powerful, irrational, and violent emotion.

Also widely used throughout the Roman Empire were small sheets of gold, silver, or bronze known as *lamellae*, or "leaves," which were inscribed with spells (nearly always in Greek, although sometimes in Hebrew or Aramaic), rolled up, and worn for protection. Many served as cures for medical ailments, including migraine and fever, while others sought to influence legal proceedings (see plates 4–7) or protect from demonic harm.

During the second century CE, a new type of amulet appeared that quickly became fashionable, typically worn as a ring or a pendant. Probably first manufactured in Egypt in a Greek-Egyptian workshop,

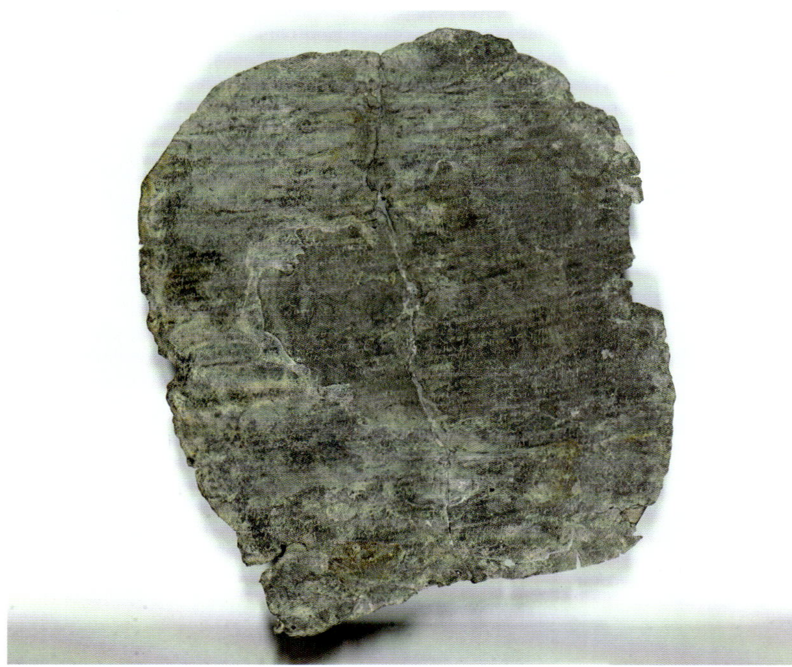

FIG. 4
Tablet with homoerotic
love charm, 3rd–4th
centuries CE

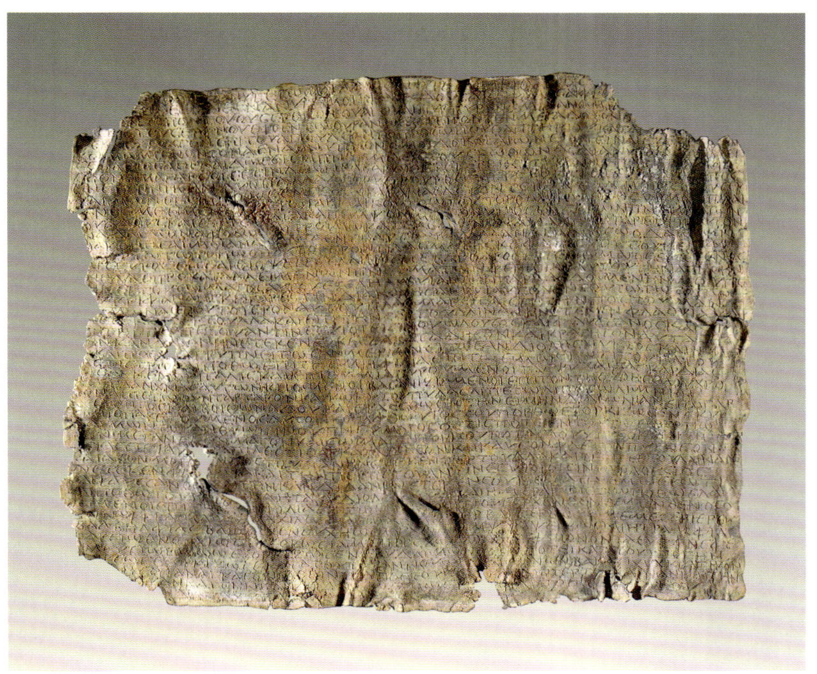

FIG. 5
Love charm for four
women, 3rd century CE

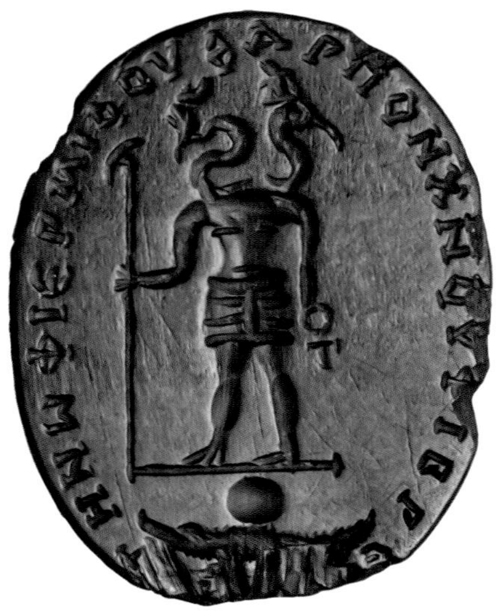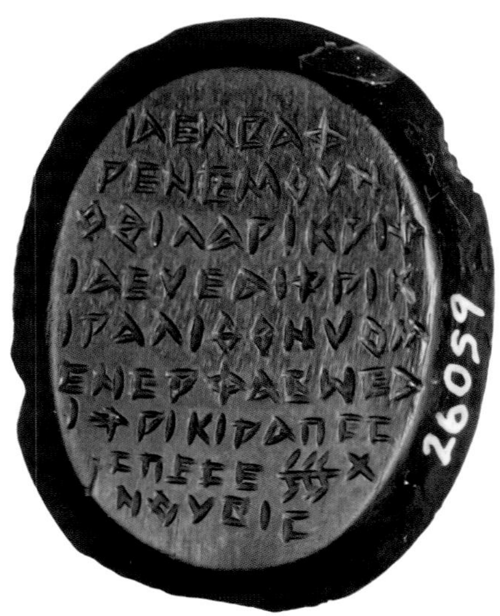

Magical gem with double-headed deity, 2nd–3rd centuries CE

these amulets were carved from semiprecious stones—mostly colorful varieties of quartz, but sometimes more unusual stones believed to have special powers, such as lapis lazuli and the metallic iron oxide hematite. They were engraved with both Egyptian and Greek deities, as well as fantastic magical figures previously unknown to the Greeks and Romans. Typically, these amulets displayed magical names and phrases similar to those found in the papyri, written in Greek. Aside from the Egyptian gods Harpocrates, Osiris, Anubis, and Serapis, who are depicted frequently, unusual deities are shown, such as a figure with two heads, one a serpent and the other an ibis, who is likely an astrological deity (fig. 6). Hekate, the Greek goddess of the Underworld and magic, also appears, sometimes with a cow's head (fig. 7). A popular variety of amulet bears the image of a lion-headed serpent, who is named by the accompanying inscription as Chnoubis, an Egyptian astrological deity believed to have influence over human health, particularly ailments of the stomach (fig. 8). Another unusual figure, known only from the magical gems, takes the form of a soldier with a rooster's head and snakes for legs, who holds a shield and a whip (fig. 9). The identity of the creature is uncertain, although it has been suggested that he is a manifestation of the sun god, or perhaps even the Jewish god Yahweh.

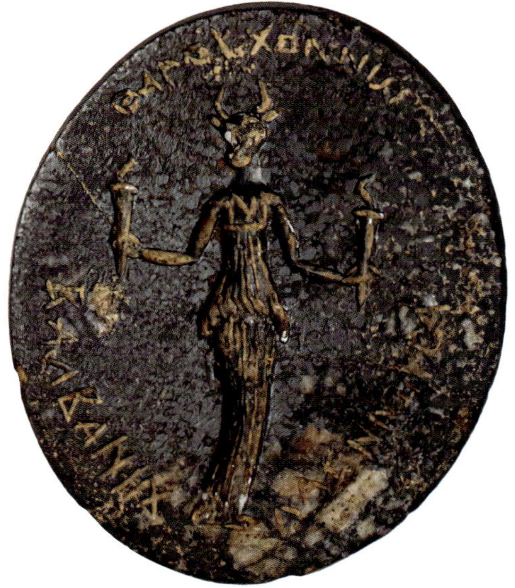
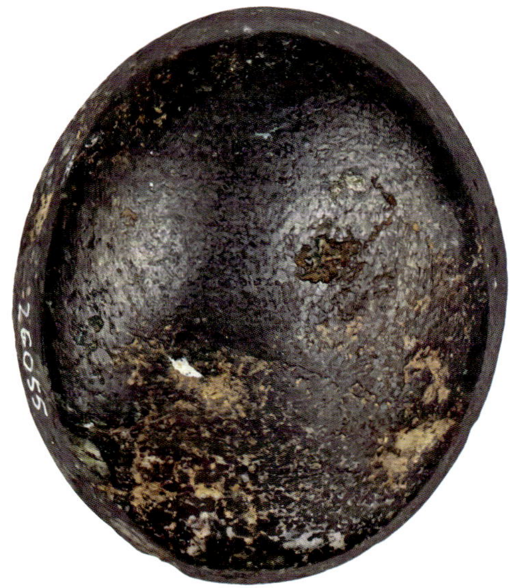

FIG. 7
Magical gem with cow-
headed Hekate, 2nd–3rd
centuries CE

How these magical practices spread throughout the Roman
Empire is not entirely clear, but the large number of surviving
amulets indicates a widespread belief that they were indeed effective.
The influence of Egyptian magic likely began soon after the Roman
conquest of the country in 30 BCE, when some Egyptian priests
found favor in the imperial court. A certain Chaeremon, who is
described both as an Egyptian priest and a Stoic philosopher, served
as tutor to the future emperor Nero in the years around 50 CE and
wrote several books on Egyptian history and culture (now lost).
Somewhat later, around 172–174 CE, another Egyptian priest, named
Harnouphis, accompanied the emperor Marcus Aurelius on a military
campaign across the Danube River to fight the Quadi tribe and is
credited with miraculously calling on the god Hermes for rain, thus
saving the troops.[4] A spell in a magical papyrus relates that a high
priest from Heliopolis named Pakhrates (or Pancrates) revealed
magical spells to the emperor Hadrian (114–138 CE).[5]

Jewish beliefs were also introduced to Rome at this time and
contributed significantly to this new magical tradition, as can be
seen not only by the use of divine names but also in the introduction
of the notions of evil demons, who could harm or possess humans
and needed to be exorcised, typically with the assistance of particular

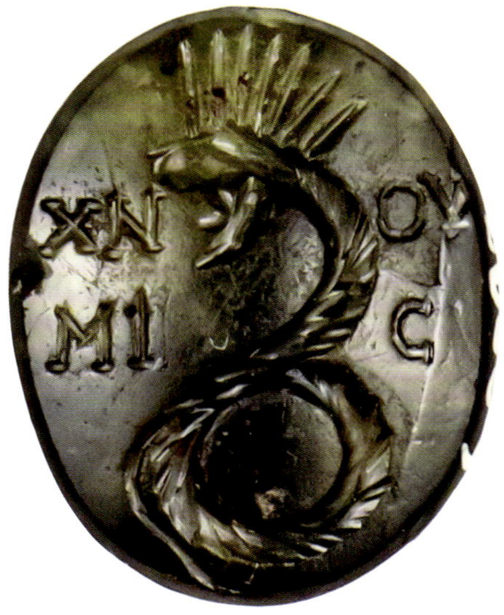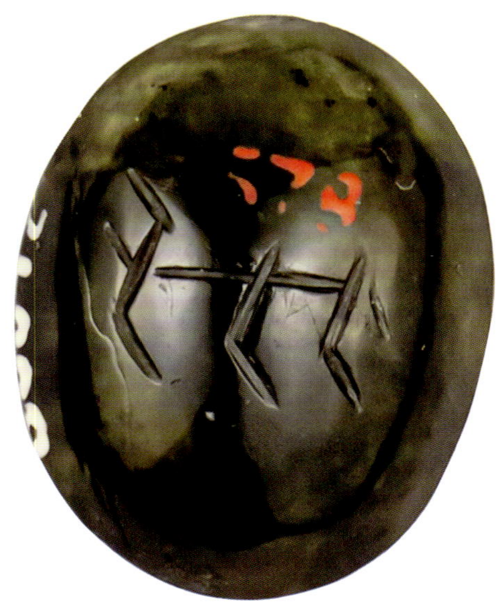

angels. This was a worldview that had been unknown to the Greeks but became widely accepted after the first century CE. The New Testament, for example, tells of itinerant Jewish exorcists at Ephesus, in Asia Minor, at the time of the apostle Paul's visit around 54 CE.[6] The seven sons of the high priest Sceva unsuccessfully attempted to invoke the name of Jesus in order to exorcise a demon from an afflicted man: "The evil spirit answered them, 'Jesus I know, and Paul I recognize, but who are you?'" The same passage also reveals that many magical books were in private hands, for after Paul converted many residents of the city to Christianity, "a number who had practiced sorcery brought their scrolls together and burned them publicly. When they calculated the value of the scrolls, the total came to fifty thousand drachmas."[7] Another story is related by the Jewish writer Flavius Josephus. Following the suppression of the Jewish revolt against Rome in 66–70 CE, the future emperor Vespasian, at that time the general in command of the war in Jerusalem, witnessed an exorcism by a man named Eleazar, who used a magic ring and a root said to have been prescribed by King Solomon.[8] It is through encounters such as this that the Greeks and Romans in the empire learned of the belief in demonic possession.

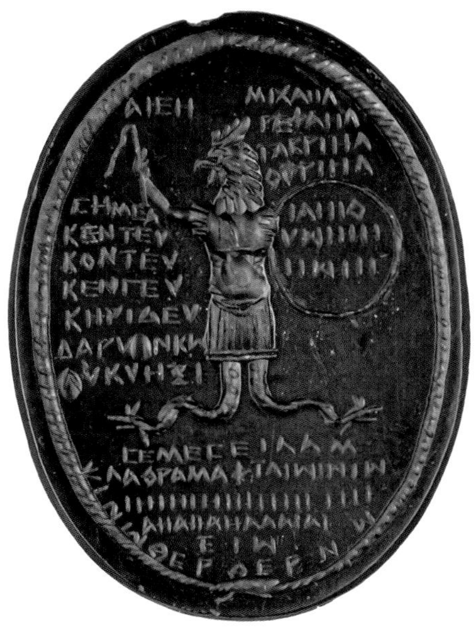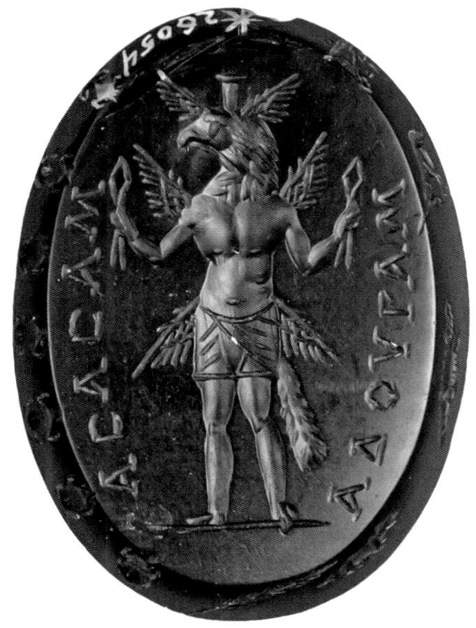

Not everyone, however, was a believer in magic. Around 170 CE, the Greek-speaking Syrian satirist Lucian composed *Philospeudes* (*The Lover of Lies*), which humorously ridicules magical beliefs.[9] His protagonist in the work, Tychiades, tells of a recent meeting with his highly educated philosopher friends in which he is shocked and exasperated to learn how credulous they are. Each of the friends in turn narrates a supernatural experience, beginning with superstitious medical cures and a debate about the efficaciousness of incantations for healing (including swearing to the effectiveness of a Babylonian magician) and continuing with an anecdote about a love charm enacted by a Hyperborean magician, an exorcism of an evil spirit by a (probably Jewish) Syrian from Palestine, statues that come to life at night, an encounter with the Underworld goddess Hekate, the appearance of ghosts, a haunted house purged by reading from Egyptian magical books, and an encounter with an Egyptian holy man named Pancrates, a teacher with miraculous powers (and likely the same individual named in the magical papyrus as the Pakhrates who met Emperor Hadrian). All the magical practices in these stories, about which Lucian appears to have been well informed, reflect actual magical beliefs, as known from many literary sources of the time, including the magical papyri themselves.

Magical gem with snake-legged deity, 2nd–3rd centuries CE

The belief in magic was clearly pervasive. Curse tablets and magical gems survive in the thousands and have been found in all parts of the empire. Roman literature is full of stories of wandering magicians and local sorceresses, who practiced their trade. A group of lead curse tablets from the Agora of Athens dating from the third century CE were all written by the same scribe, who appears to have set up shop there.[10] Some individuals, such as Lucian, ridiculed these beliefs, and many considered magical practices to be irreligious and improper. Sometimes the professional magicians fell afoul of the civic authorities and were expelled from Rome or even executed.[11] Roman historians note that such expulsions and prosecutions occurred periodically, although evidently aimed primarily at astrologers who presumed to forecast the future (thus threatening imperial authority) rather than magicians who made amulets. Most respectable citizens likely disapproved of magic and viewed its practice as immoral, despite the apparent ease in finding working magicians.

The conversion of the Roman Empire to Christianity in the fourth century CE hardly changed the popular belief in magic, despite the frequent condemnation by Christian theologians of such practices. Indeed, in Jewish, Christian, and Islamic culture throughout the Middle Ages there was a widespread acceptance of the presence of angels and demons in everyday life and the efficacy of magical amulets. Books of magic continued to circulate and were widely copied in Greek, Latin, Hebrew, and Arabic. The old magical spells often remained unchanged, although sometimes they were Christianized to be less offensive to the religious authorities, with appeals to Christ, the Virgin, saints, and angels, whose names replaced those of the pagan deities of former times. Thanks largely to the intellectual curiosity of educated monks and scholars in the monasteries and royal courts of Europe and Byzantium, ancient magical beliefs were transmitted to the modern world.[12]

1. See Korshi Dosoo, "A History of the Theban Magical Library," *Bulletin of the American Society of Papyrologists* 53 (2016): 251–74.

2. PDM xiv.103–12; Hans Dieter Betz, ed., *The Greek Magical Papyri in Translation Including the Demotic Spells* (University of Chicago Press, 1986), 201; Jacco Dieleman, *Priests, Tongues, and Rites: The London-Leiden Magical Manuscripts and Translation in Egyptian Ritual (100–300 CE)* (Brill, 2005), 123–26 and 313–14.

3. PGM CXXX; Betz, *Greek Magical Papyri*, 323.

4. Cassius Dio, *Roman History* 71.8.4, calls the Egyptian a magician.

5. PGM IV.2446–2455; Betz, *Greek Magical Papyri*, 83.

6. Acts 19:11–20.

7. Acts 19:19.

8. Josephus, *Antiquities of the Jews* 8.42–49.

9. See Daniel Ogden, *In Search of the Sorcerer's Apprentice: The Traditional Tales of Lucian's* Lover of Lies (Classical Press of Wales, 2007). The episode of the Egyptian priest Pancrates includes the original version of the story "The Sorcerer's Apprentice."

10. D. R. Jordan, "Defixiones from a Well Near the Southwest Corner of the Athenian Agora," *Hesperia* 54 (1985): 205–55.

11. Matthew Dickie, *Magic and Magicians in the Greco-Roman World* (Routledge, 2001), 185–94.

12. See, for example, the extensive collection of magical books in the library of the Benedictine Abbey of St. Augustine in Canterbury, England, in the thirteenth century (Sophie Page, *Magic in the Cloister: Pious Motives, Illicit Interests, and Occult Approaches to the Medieval Universe* [Pennsylvania State University Press, 2013]: 5–30) and the copies of Greek magical books dating from the fifteenth to nineteenth centuries that preserve much earlier material (Armand Delatte, *Anecdota atheniensia; Tome I: Textes grecs inédits relatifs à l'histoire des religions* [H. Vaillant-Carmanne and E. Champion, 1927]).

Plates

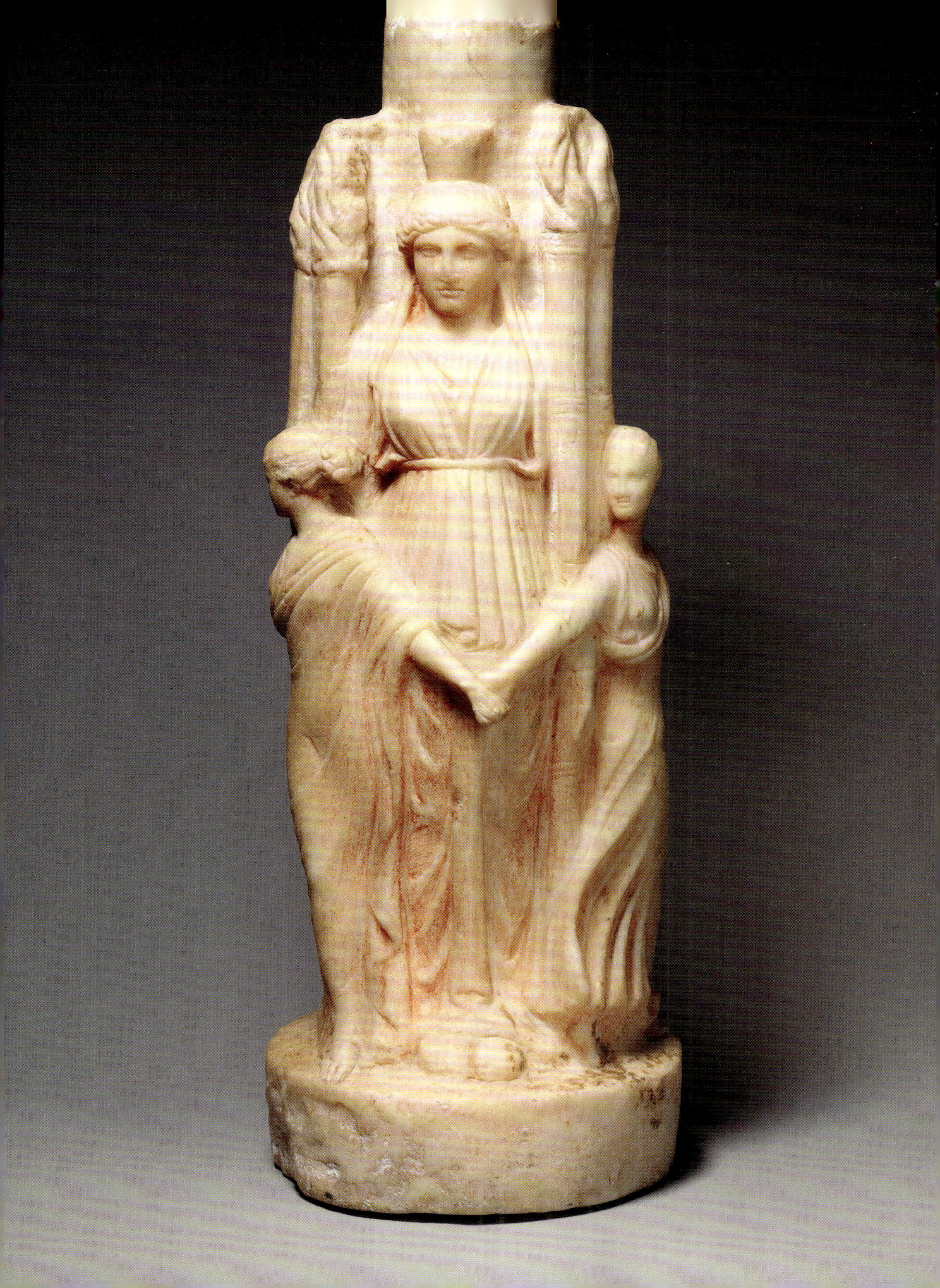

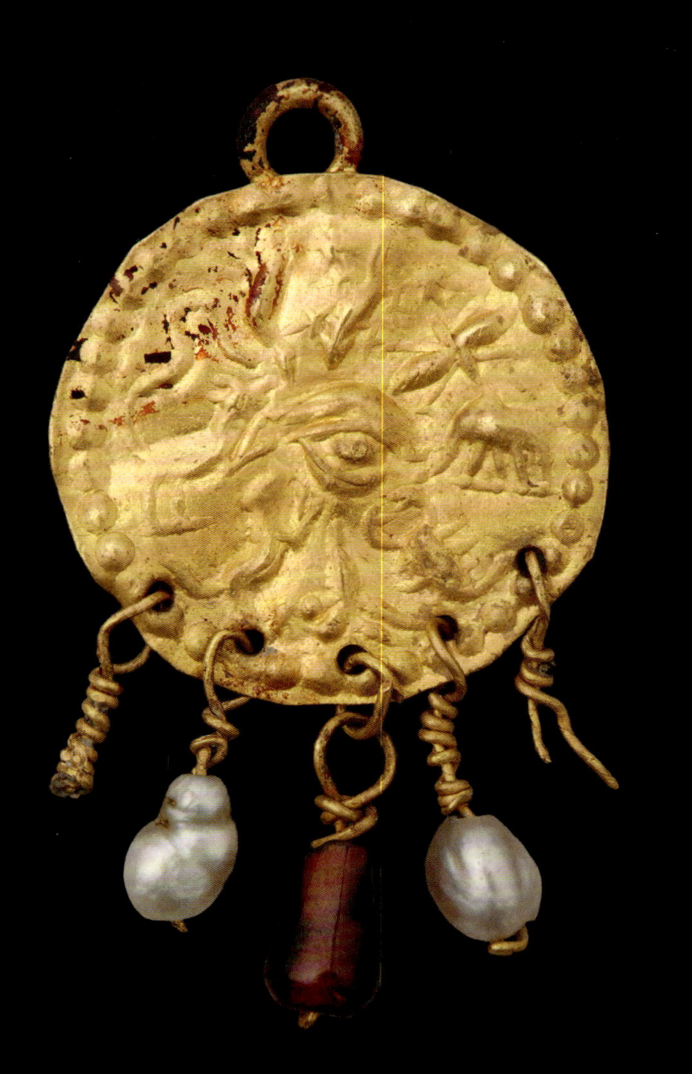

PLATE 2
Pendant amulet against the evil eye,
2nd century CE

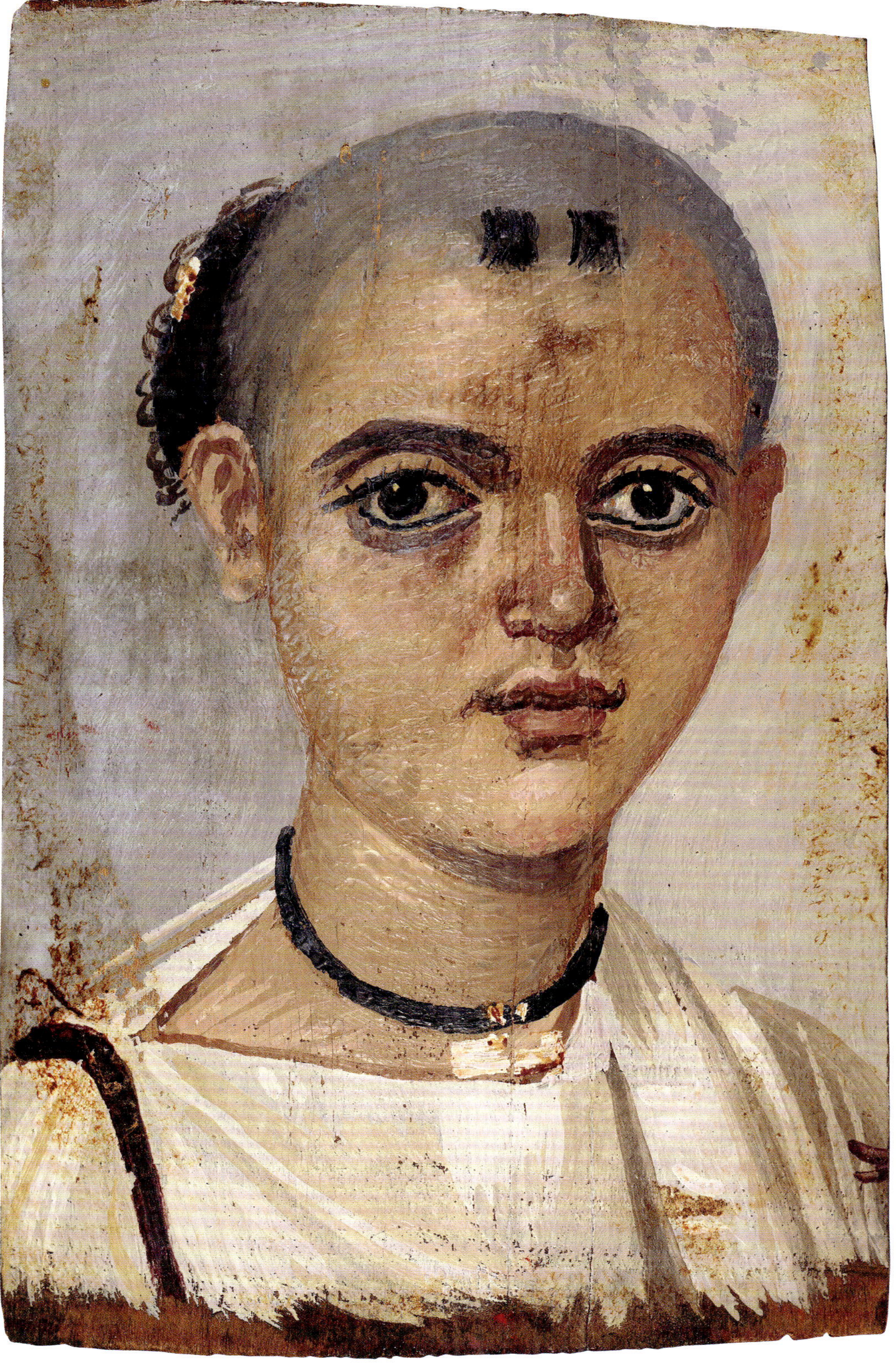

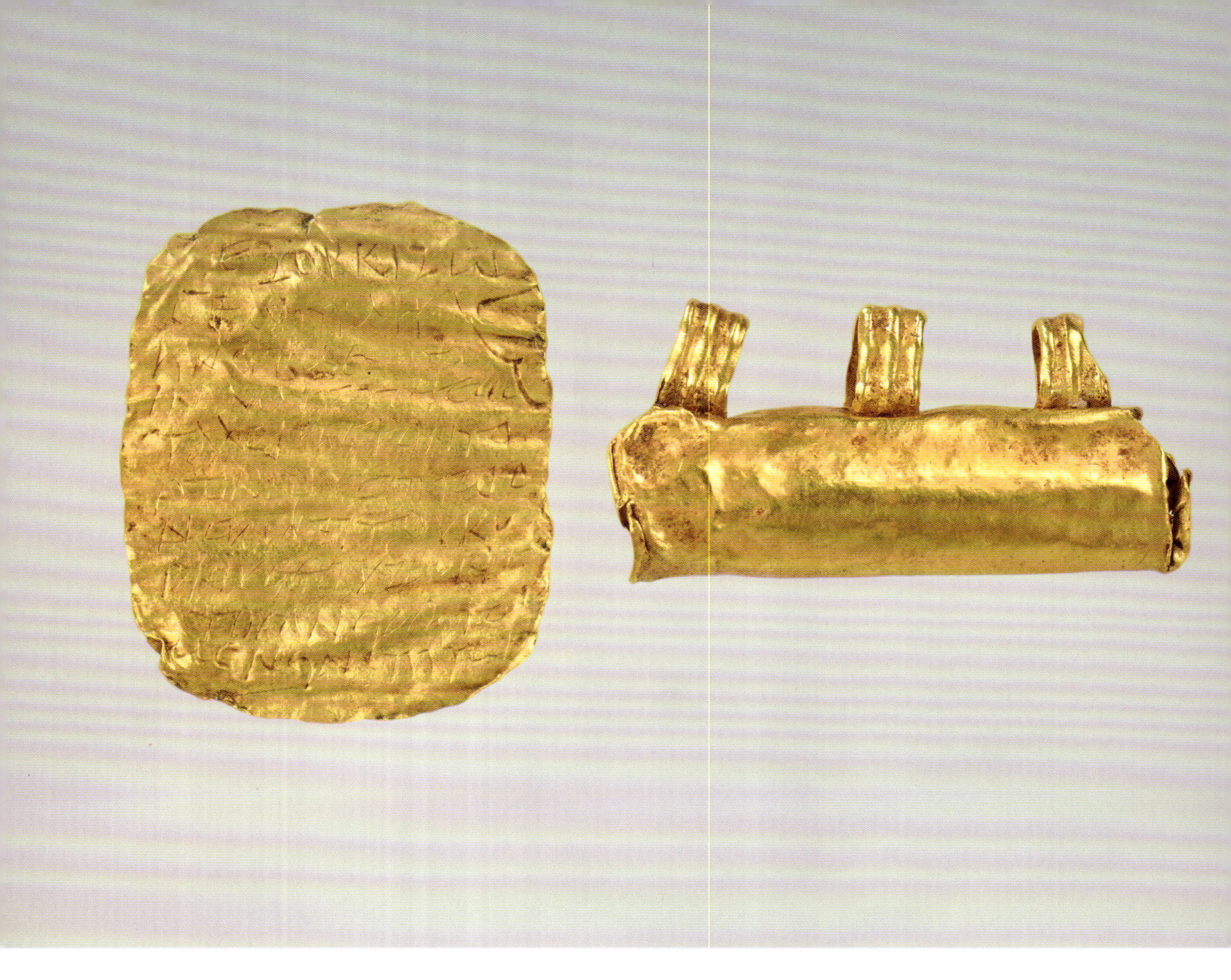

PLATE 4
Womb amulet and case, 1st century CE

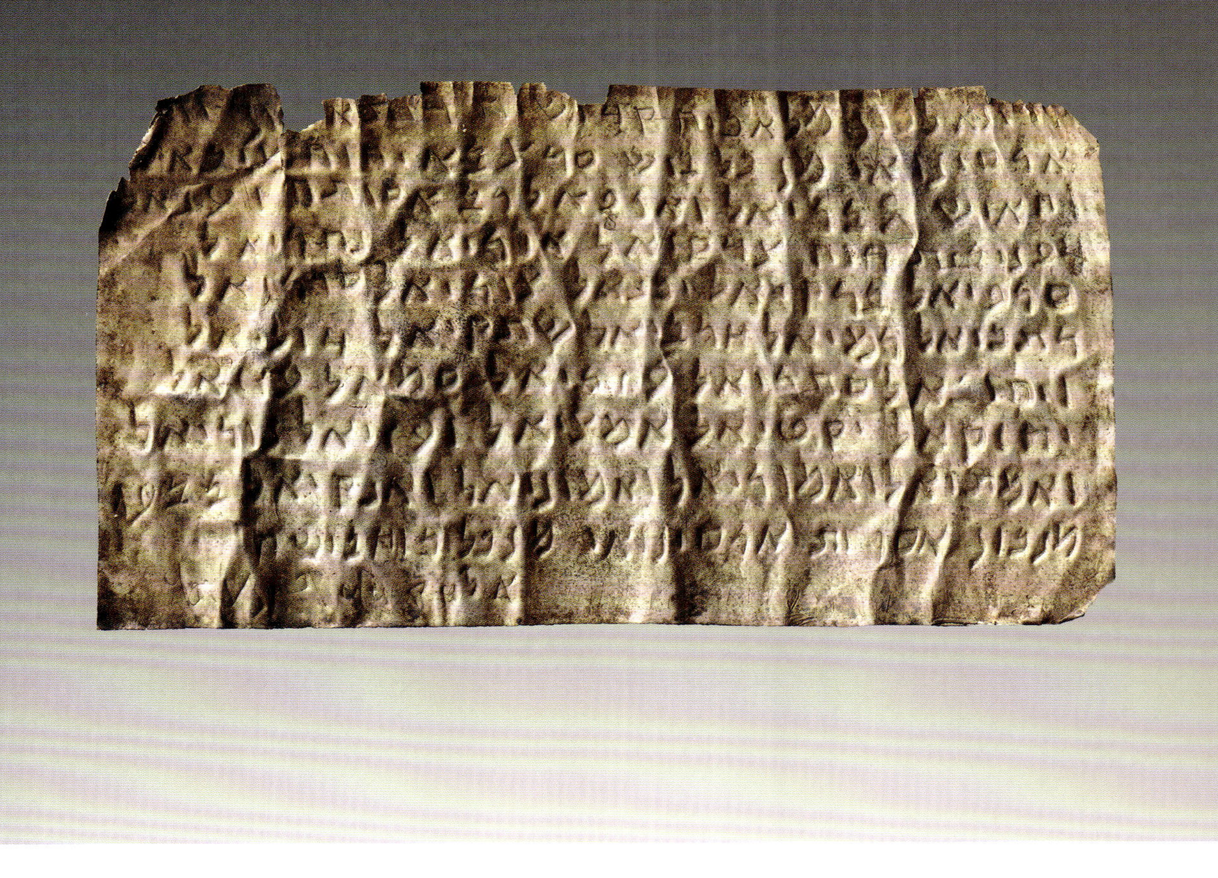

PLATE 5
Jewish amulet invoking angels,
3rd century CE

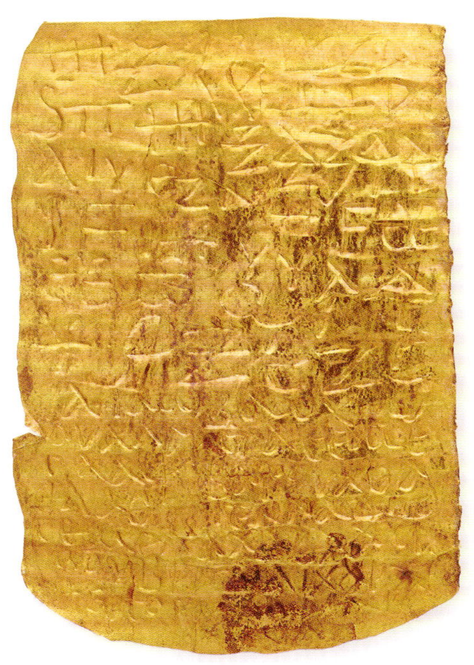

PLATE 6
Protective amulet and case,
mid-3rd century CE

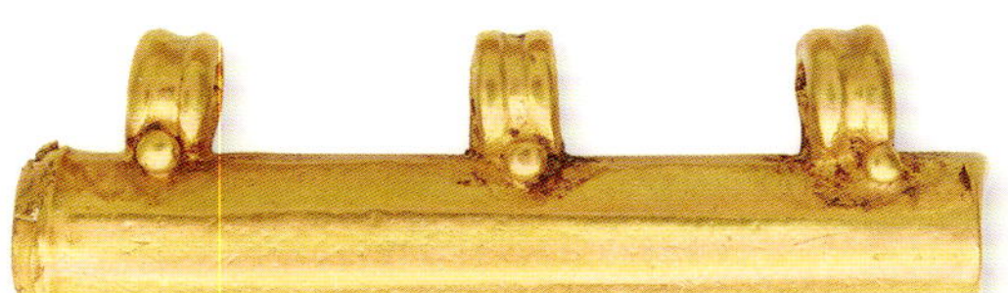

PLATE 7
Amulet to influence a legal case,
4th century CE

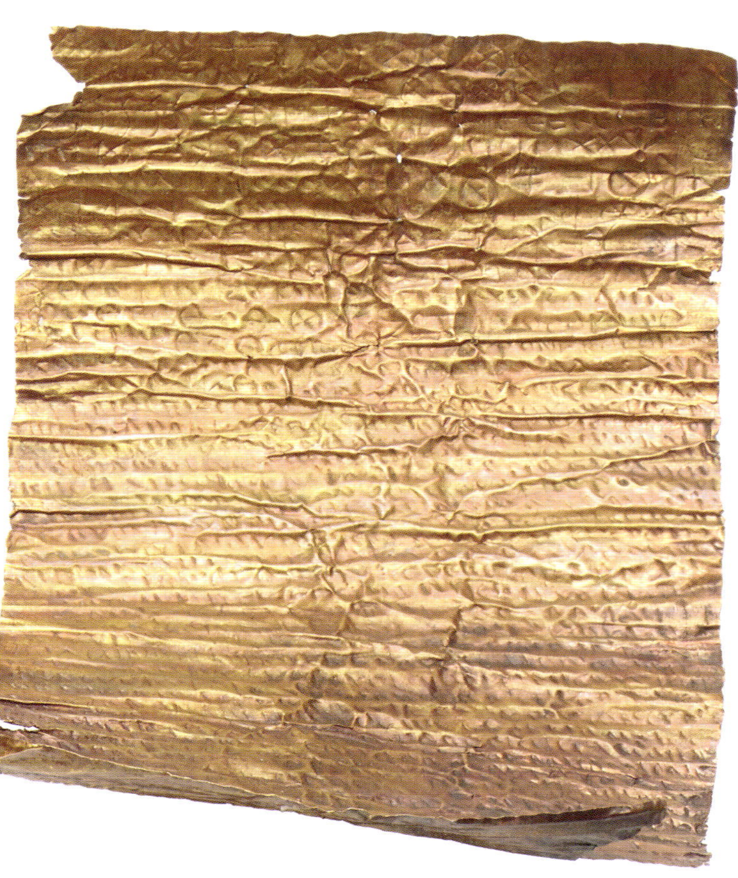

PLATE 9
Papyrus with a magician's monologue,
2nd–3rd centuries CE

CΠICTOYΚΩΝ . . ΜΝΗΚΕ
ΧΡΩΩΚΑΤΑ . . . CEΙΚΩΝ
ΚΡΩΩΛΟC . . ωΤΗΝΤωC
ΡΟΝΗΝΥ . ΟΜΕΝΕΙΚΩΝ
ΔΤΗ . ΩC . . . ΗΝΗΜ . .
ΡICTOΦωC . . ΟΚΑΠΕ . . .
ΤΗ ΚΩΝ ΤΑ . . . . ΟΙCω
ΤΗΝ ΘΑΛΑΤΤ . Ν . ΤΟ . ΕΙ
Ν CωC ΚΩΝ . . . . . ΘΙC
. . . ICΕΘΕC . . . CωΤΗ
ΕΙΟΝΟΝ Ο . ΧΕ . ΡICΚΩΝ ΦΑΡ
ΕΡΑΚΗ Ο ΠΟΤΑ . . ΕΖΩΝ . . .
ΝΟΝ ΟΥΠΑ . . ΛΑ . ΛΑ . ΝΩ . ΝΙΝ
ΗΤΗ ΜΟΡΦΟΒΟ . ΥΜΗΝΗΤΟΝ
ΘΕΟ . ΠΟΥCΑΡ . ΩΝΛΑΤΙΤΧΗ
ΙΕΟΖ . . . ΑΥΤΗ . . . . ωΕCΟ . . Ν
CΟΤΕΠΙΠΙΝΟC . ω ΧΡΗΠΛΘΗ
ΘΕ . . . ΦΟΙΝΕCΛ . . ΡΟ . ΤΙΩΝ
ΩΡΙΚΩΟΝΕ . . . . . Ω . ΟΝΙC
ΤΙCΚΛΙ . . . . Ι ΠΑΡΑΔΟ
CΟΝΑΝΔΙCΔΟΚΕ . . . .
ΦΟ . ΙΠ . . ΡΟΟ . C . . . . ΡΑΛΗ
ΝΕCΩ . . . . ΝΙCω

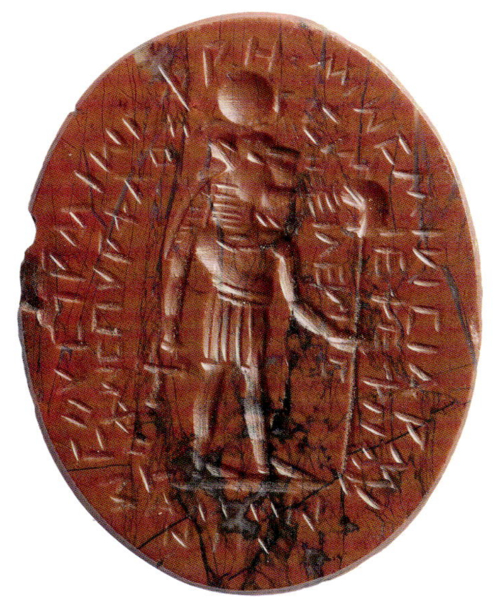
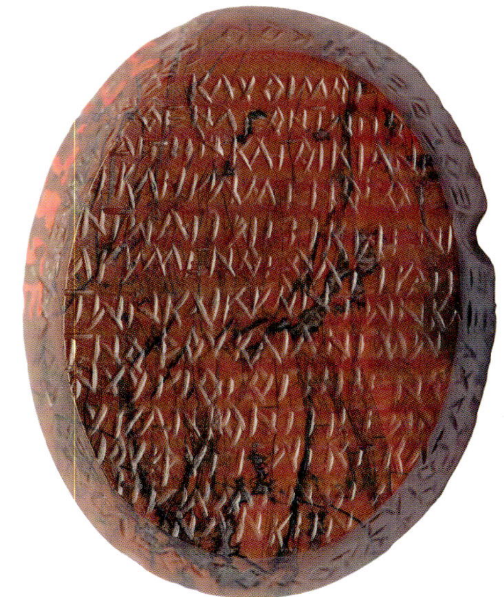

OBVERSE

REVERSE

PLATE 10
Magical gem with the god Mios,
2nd–3rd centuries CE

PLATE 11
Magical gem with Osiris,
2nd–3rd centuries CE

PLATE 12
Magical gem with Serapis,
2nd–3rd centuries CE

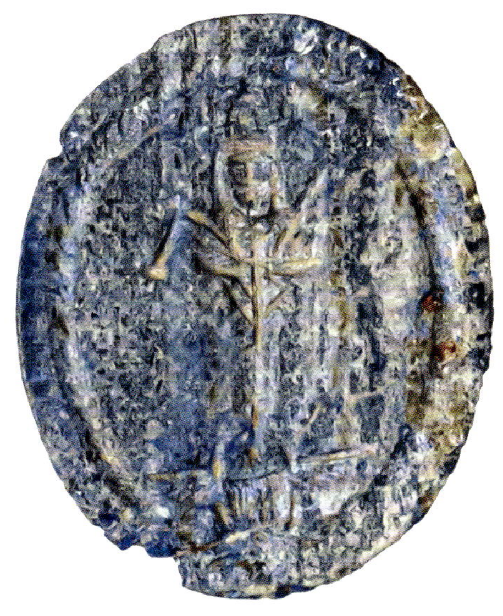

OBVERSE

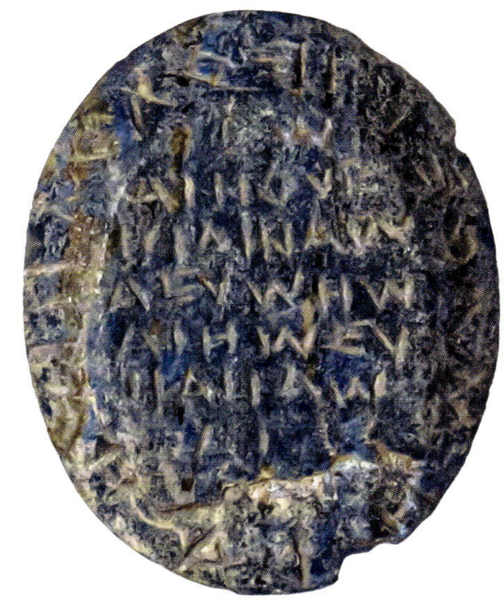

REVERSE

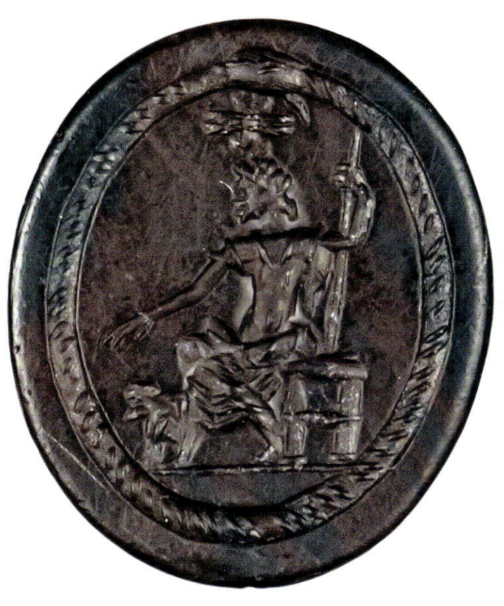

OBVERSE

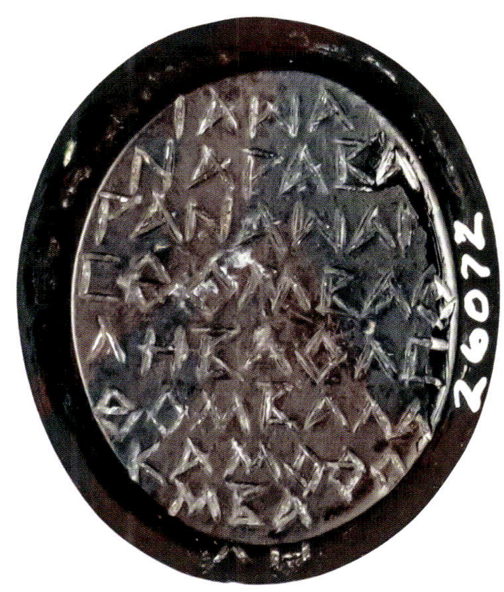

REVERSE

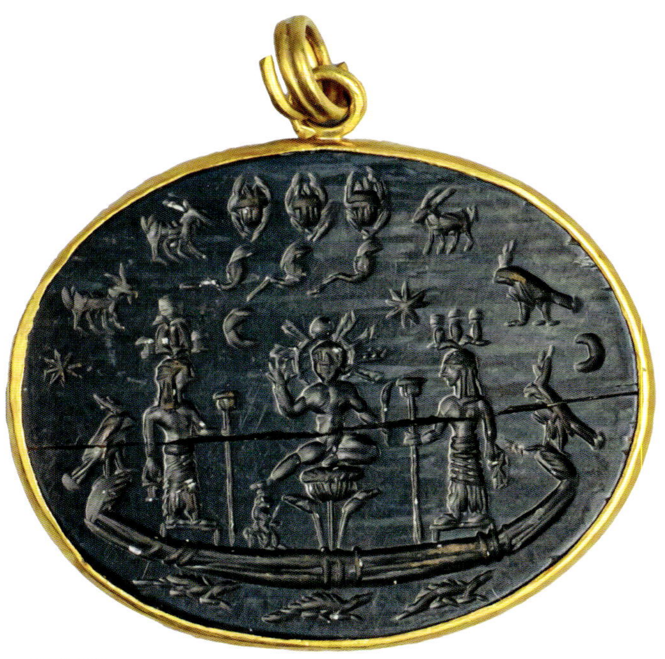

OBVERSE

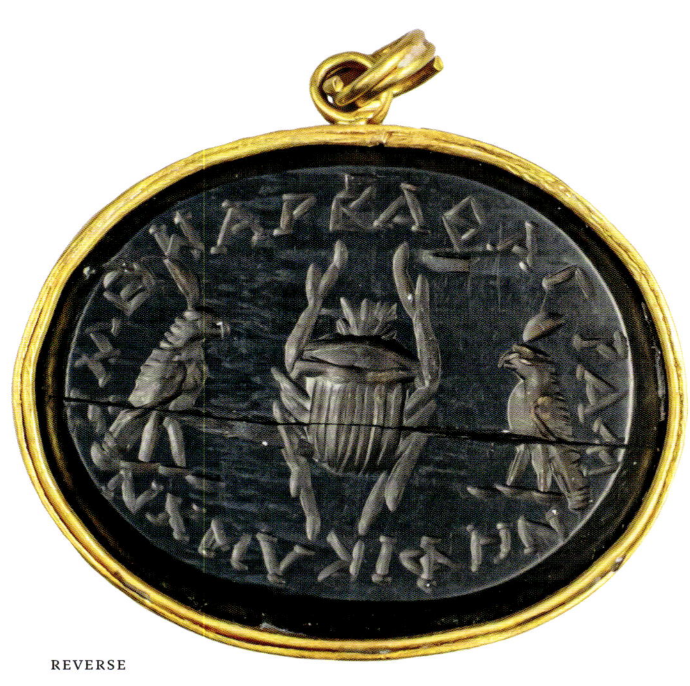

REVERSE

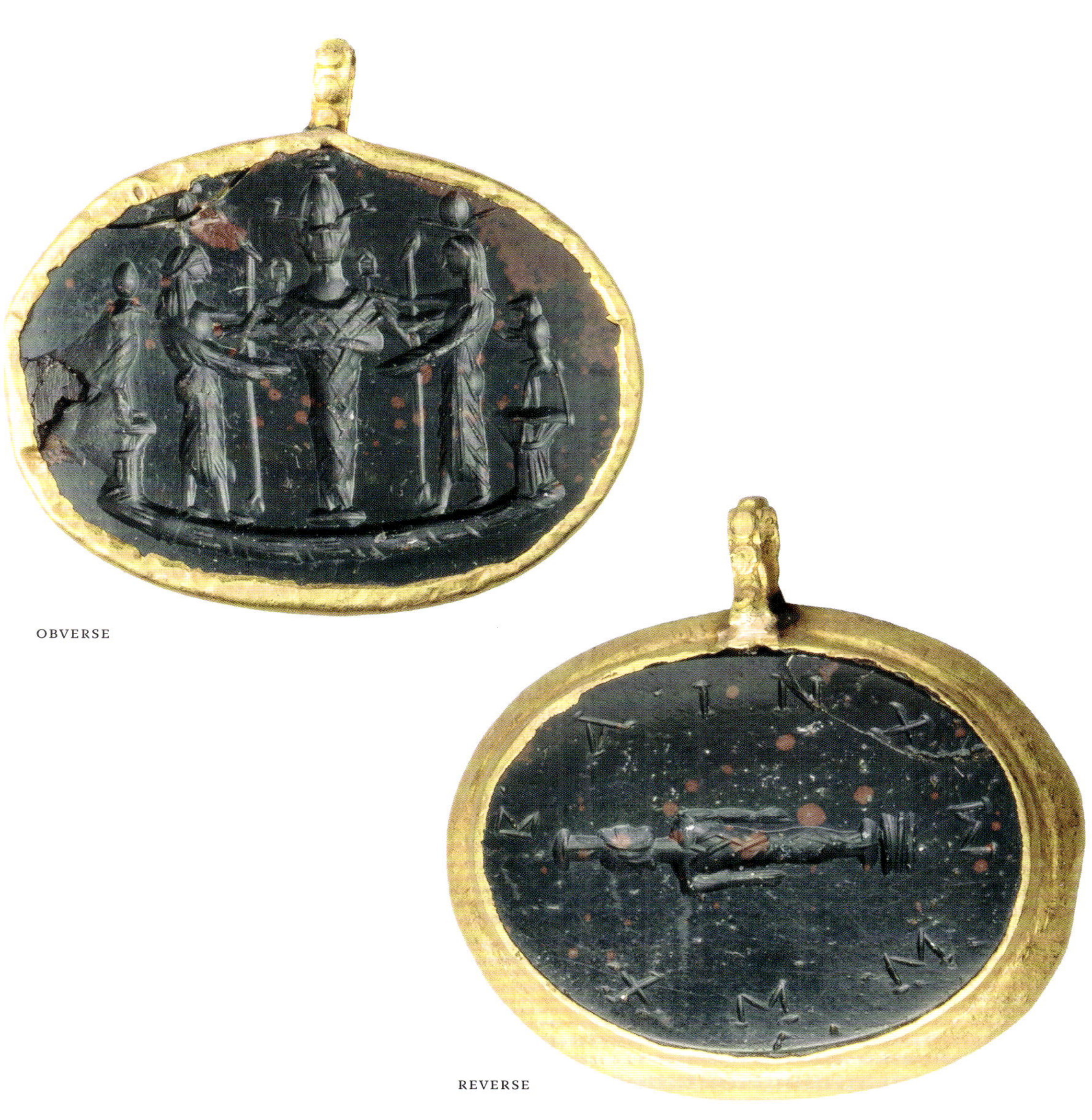

OBVERSE

REVERSE

PLATE 13
Magical gem with Harpocrates on solar boat, 2nd–3rd centuries CE

PLATE 14
Magical gem with Osiris, Isis, and Nephthys, 2nd–3rd centuries CE

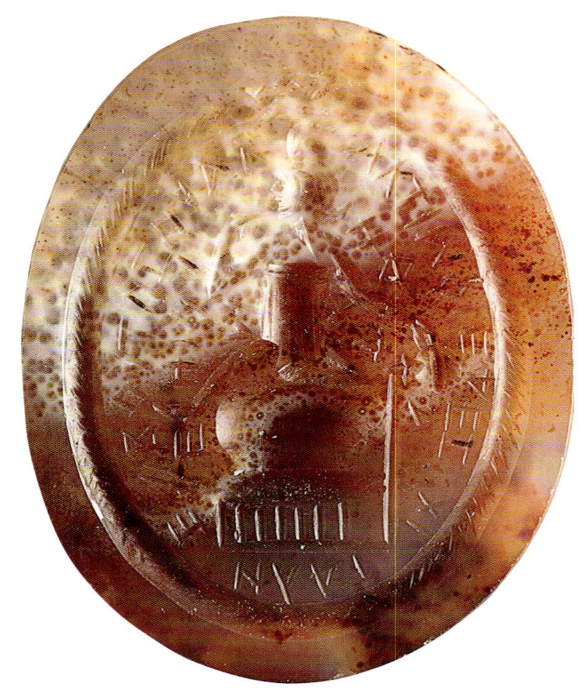

OBVERSE

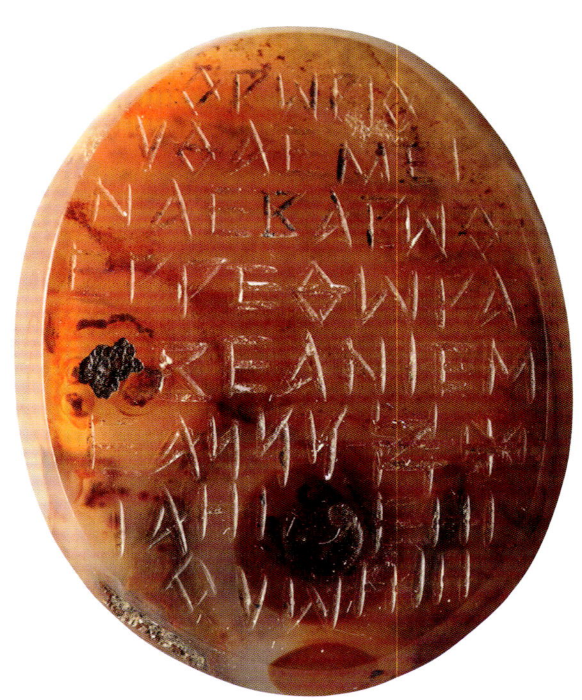

REVERSE

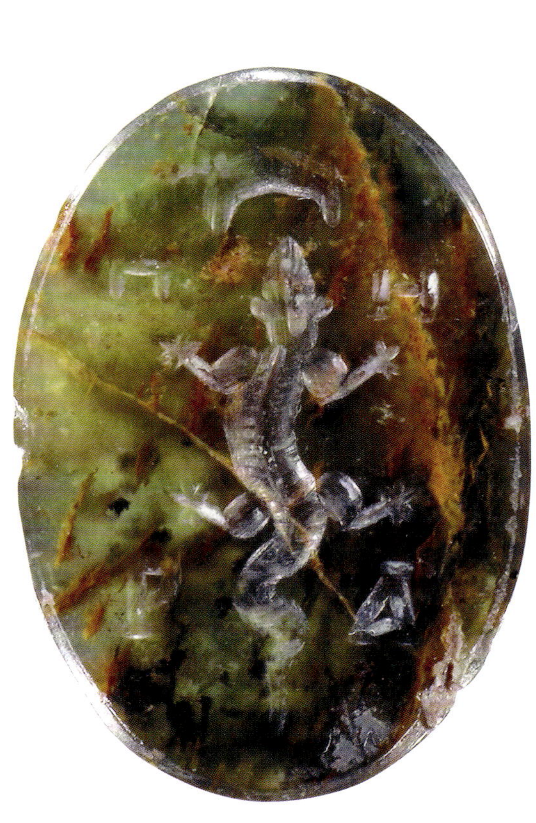

OBVERSE

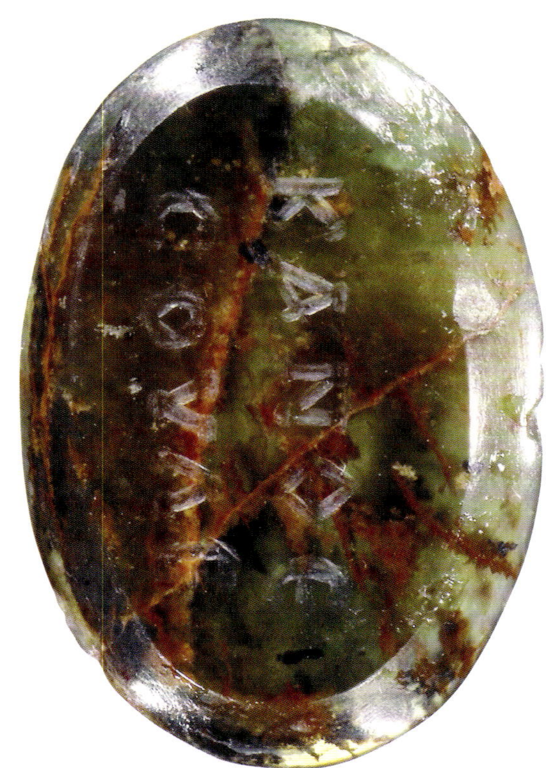

REVERSE

PLATE 16
Magical gem with lizard,
2nd–3rd centuries CE

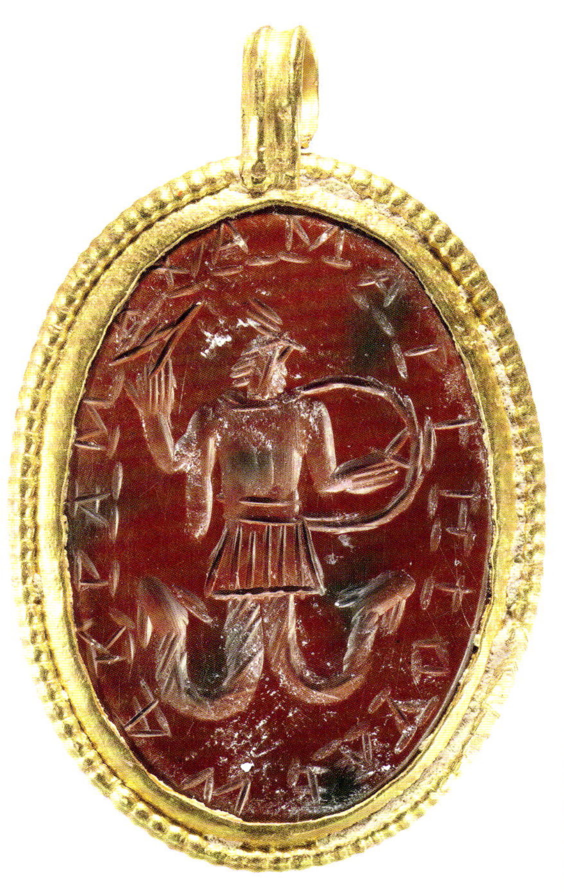

OBVERSE

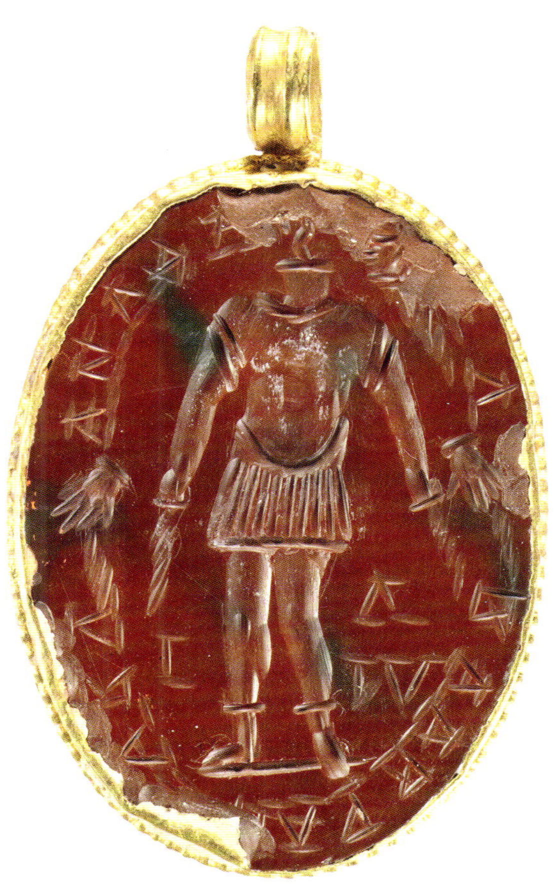

REVERSE

PLATE 17
Magical gem with cock-headed anguipede,
2nd–3rd centuries CE

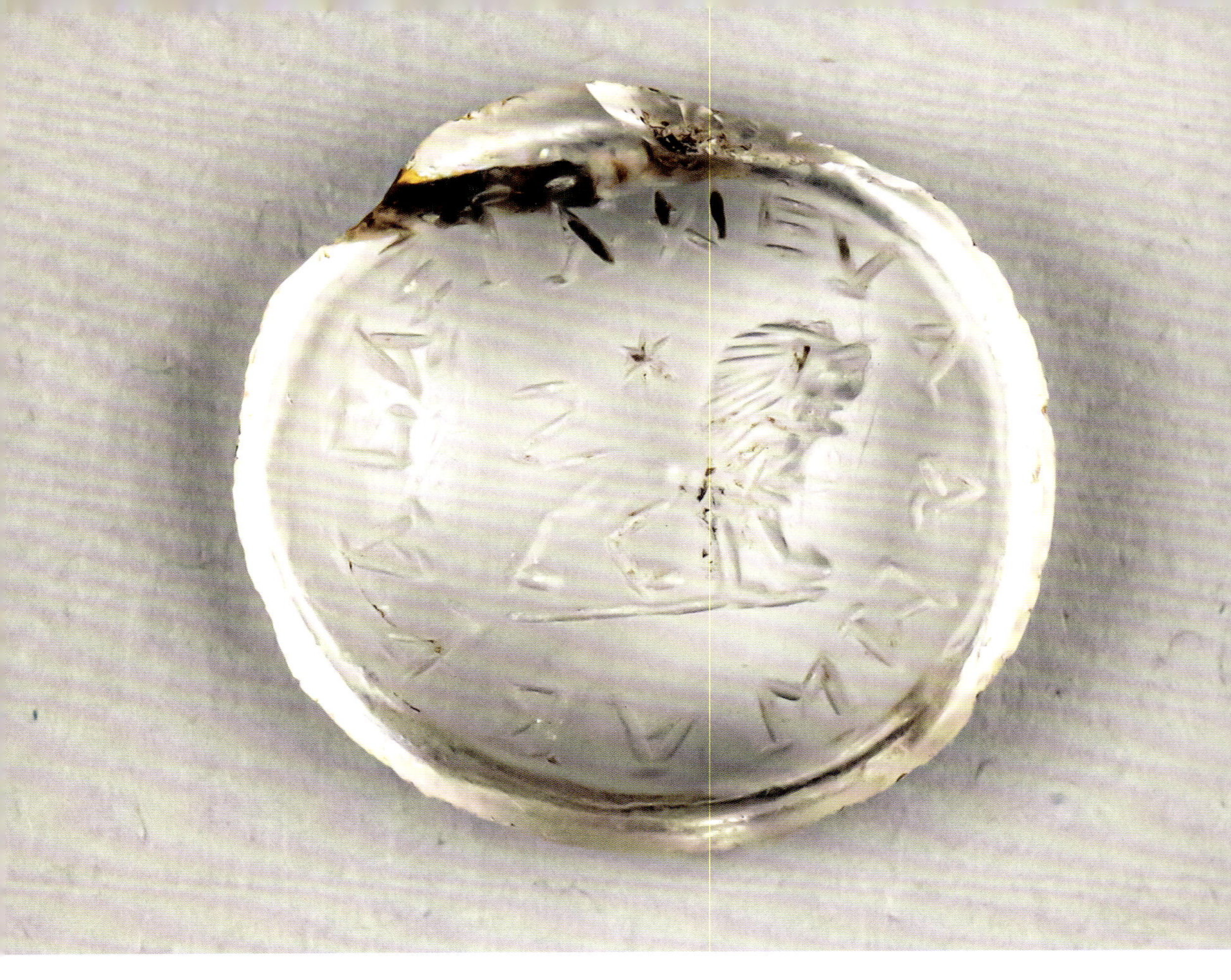

PLATE 18
Magical gem with lion, 2nd–3rd
centuries CE

96

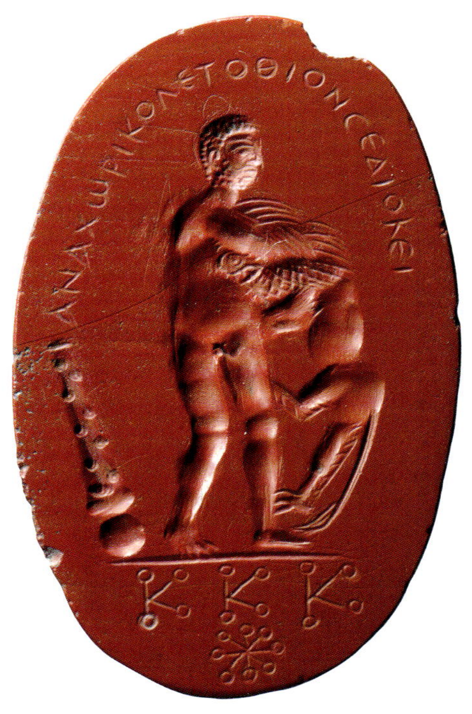

OBVERSE

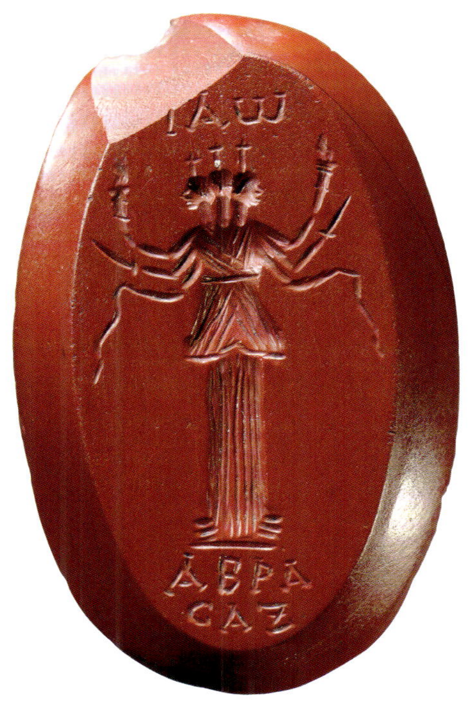

REVERSE

PLATE 19
Magical gem with Herakles and the
Nemean Lion, 2nd–3rd centuries CE

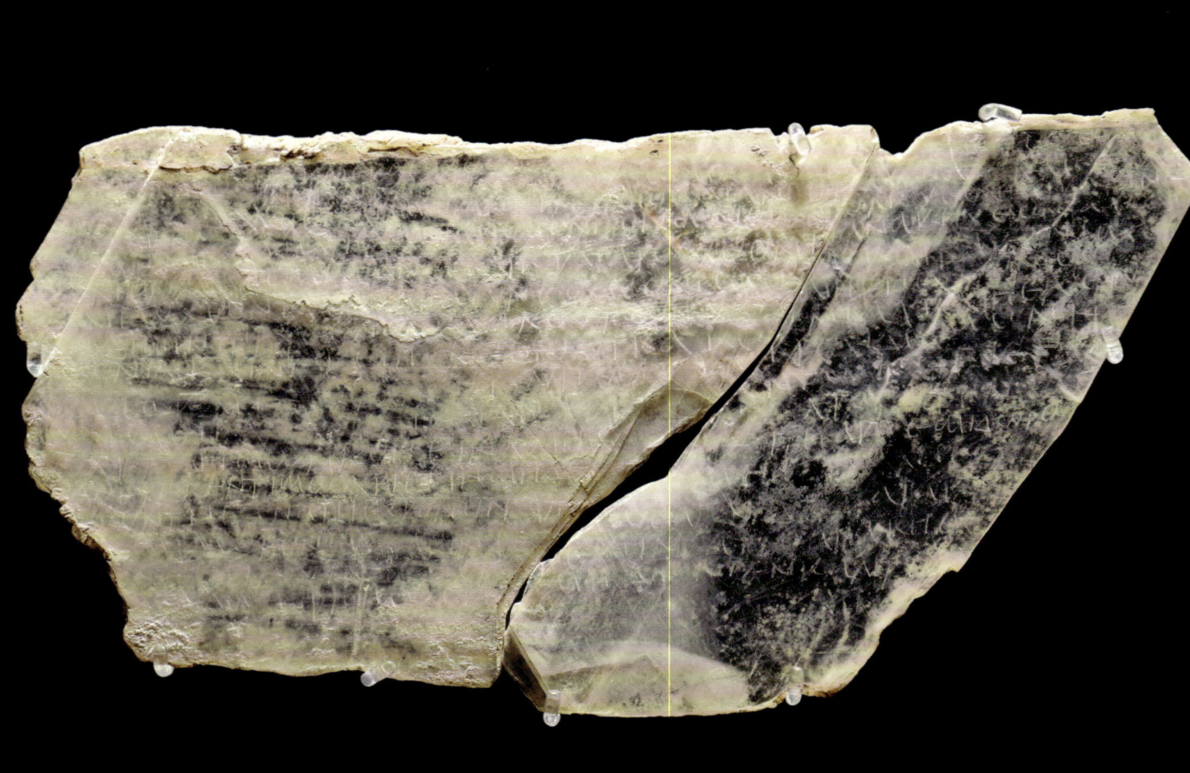

PLATE 20
Curse tablet, 3rd century CE

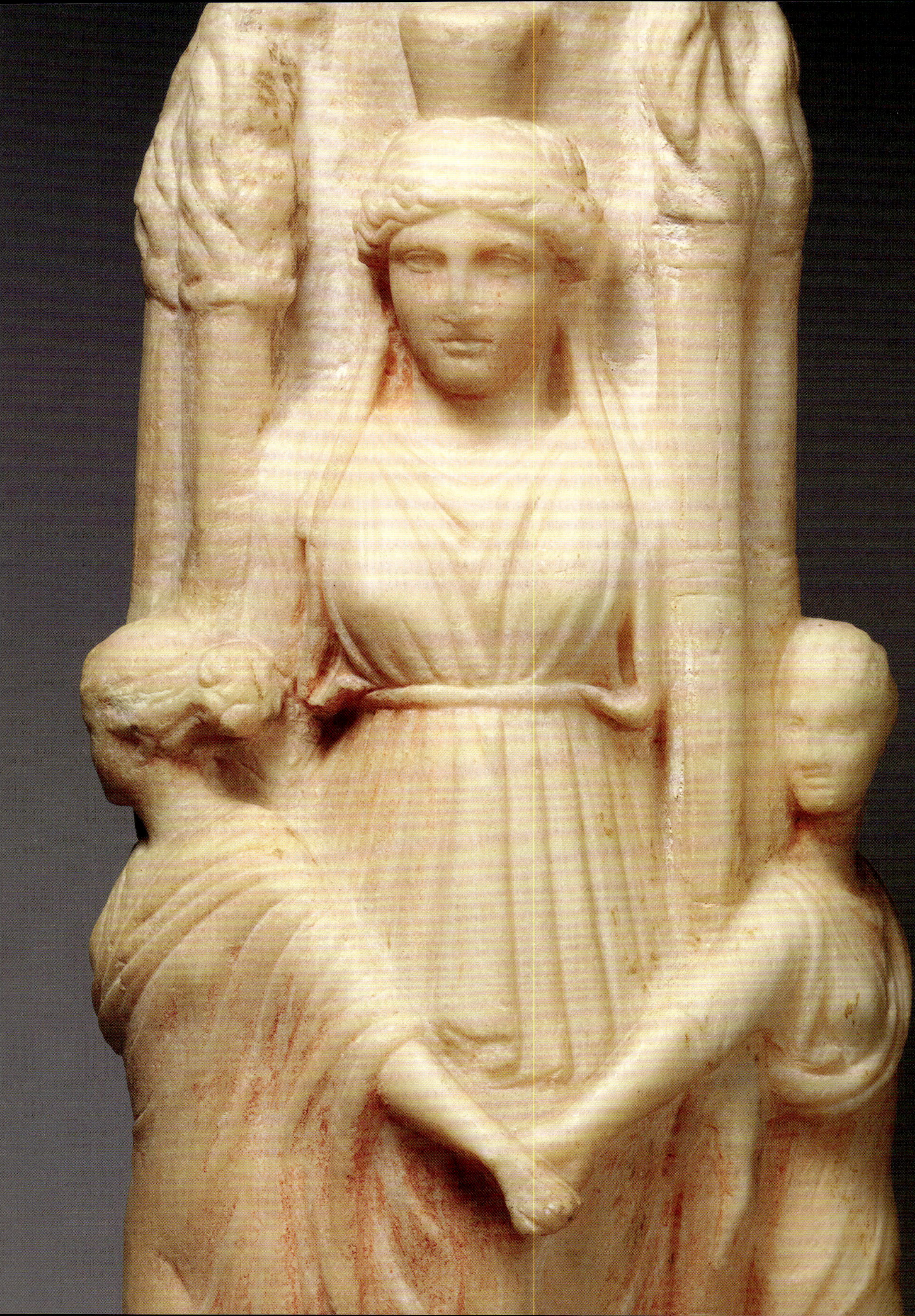

Exhibition Checklist

EGYPT

Bowl with a letter to the dead
Egyptian, Old Kingdom, about 2200 BCE
Clay; diameter: 7 ⅝ in. (19.5 cm)
From Qau, Egypt
UCL Petrie Museum of Egyptian and Suda-
nese Archaeology, University College London,
LDUCE-UC16163
Page 25, figure 12

Magic wand depicting a procession of deities
Egyptian, Middle Kingdom, late 12th–13th Dynasty,
about 1880–1700 BCE
Hippopotamus ivory; 6 ⁵⁄₁₆ × 14 ⅜ × ¼ in.
(16 × 36.5 × 0.7 cm)
Baltimore, The Walters Art Museum,
Acquired by Henry Walters, 1914, 71.510
Page 27, figure 14

Curse figure
Egyptian, Middle Kingdom, 12th Dynasty,
1991–1802 BCE
Clay with red pigment; 13 ¾ × 5 ¾ × 3 ⅝ in.
(34.8 × 14.5 × 9.3 cm)
From Saqqara, Egypt
Brussels, Musées royaux d'art et d'histoire /
Koninklijke Musea voor Kunst en Geschiedenis,
E.07442
Page 23, figure 10

Papyrus column amulet
Egyptian, 26th–30th Dynasties, 664–332 BCE
Faience; height: 5 ⅜ in. (13.7 cm), diameter: 1 ⁷⁄₁₆ in.
(3.7 cm)
New York, The Metropolitan Museum of Art, Pur-
chase, Edward S. Harkness Gift, 1926, 26.7.1036
Page 18, figure 3

Papyrus column amulet
Egyptian, 26th Dynasty, about 664–525 BCE
Amazonite; height: 2 ⅜ in. (5.9 cm), width: 1 in.
(2.4 cm)
Baltimore, Johns Hopkins Archaeological Museum,
Cohen Collection of Egyptian Antiquities, purchased
by the university, 3724
Page 18, figure 4

Wedjat amulet
Egyptian, 26th–30th Dynasties, 664–332 BCE
Faience; 1 ¹⁵⁄₁₆ × 1 ¼ in. (3.3 × 3.2 cm)
New York, The Metropolitan Museum of Art, Gift of
Helen Miller Gould, 1910, 10.130.1900
Page 19, figure 5

Set of four amulets of the sons of Horus
Egyptian, 23rd–25th Dynasties, 818–664 BCE
Faience; 3 ¼ × 1 × ¼ in. (8.3 × 2.5 × 0.6 cm)
Toledo Museum of Art, Gift of Edward Drummond
Libbey, 1906.48a–d

Papyrus column amulet
Egyptian, 26th–31st Dynasties, 664–332 BCE
Faience; 2 ⅜ × ¾ × ¾ in. (6 × 1.9 × 1.9 cm)
Toledo Museum of Art, Gift of Edward Drummond
Libbey, 1906.55a

Ankh amulet
Egyptian, 26th Dynasty, 664–525 BCE
Faience; 2 ¼ × ⅞ × ⅜ in. (5.7 × 2.2 × 0.9 cm)
Toledo Museum of Art, Gift of Edward Drummond
Libby, 1906.65

Ibis amulet
Egyptian, 25th–31st Dynasties, 747–332 BCE
Faience; ⅞ × 1 ¼ × ⅜ in. (2.2 × 3.2 × 0.9 cm)
Toledo Museum of Art, Gift of Edward Drummond
Libbey, 1906.147

Crocodile amulet
Egyptian, 25th–31st Dynasties, 747–332 BCE
Stone; ⅜ × 1 ¼ × ⅜ in. (0.9 × 3.2 × 0.9 cm)
Toledo Museum of Art, Gift of Edward Drummond
Libbey, 1906.149

Cobra amulet
Egyptian, 25th–31st Dynasties, 747–332 BCE
Faience; 2 × 1 × ¼ in. (5.1 × 2.5 × 0.6 cm)
Toledo Museum of Art, Gift of Edward Drummond
Libbey, 1906.151

Winged scarab amulet
Egyptian, 25th–31st Dynasties, 747–332 BCE
Faience; 1 × 3 ⅛ × ½ in. (2.5 × 7.9 × 1.3 cm)
Toledo Museum of Art, Gift of Florence Scott Libbey,
1925.544

Amulet of Taweret
Egyptian, 26th–30th Dynasties, 664–332 BCE
Faience; 3 ¹³⁄₁₆ × 1 ⅛ × 1 ⁵⁄₁₆ in. (9.7 × 2.9 × 3.4 cm)
New York, The Metropolitan Museum of Art, Gift of
J. Pierpont Morgan, 1917, 17.194.2236
Page 28, figure 15

Amulets from the burial of Djedmutesankh
Egyptian, 21st Dynasty, 1000–945 BCE
Gold; largest is 1 ⅜ in. (3.5 cm) tall
From Tomb MMA 60, Deir el-Bahri, Thebes, Egypt
New York, The Metropolitan Museum of Art, Rogers
Fund, 1925, 25.3.168a–d
Page 29, figure 17

Amulet plaque with sacred symbols
Egyptian, Late Period or Ptolemaic Period, 664–30 BCE
Gold; 1 ⅝ × 1 ⅜ in. (4.1 × 3.5 cm)
Said to be from Krokodilopolis (Gebelein), Egypt
New York, The Metropolitan Museum of Art, Rogers
Fund, 1924, 24.2.19

Magical stela of Horus
Egyptian, Ptolemaic Period, 332–280 BCE
Chlorite schist; 8 ¹⁄₁₆ × 4 ¾ × 1 ¾ in. (20.5 × 12 ×
4.5 cm)
New York, The Metropolitan Museum of Art, Rogers
Fund, 1920, 20.2.23
Page 22, figure 8

Papyrus with spell against demons
Egyptian, 26th Dynasty, 664–525 BCE
Papyrus and ink; 29 ¹⁵⁄₁₆ × 4 ⅞ in. (76.1 × 12.4 cm)
The Brooklyn Museum, Bequest of Theodora Wil-
bour from the collection of her father, Charles Edwin
Wilbour, 47.218.156a–d
Pages 24–25, figure 11

MESOPOTAMIA

Mask of Humbaba
Old Babylonian, 2000–1700 BCE
Fired clay; 3 ⅛ × 2 ¾ × 1 ⅛ in. (8 × 7 × 2.8 cm)
From Ur (Diqdiqqah), Iraq
London, The British Museum, 1931,1010.458
Page 39, figure 3

Amulet with the demon Lamashtu
Neo-Assyrian, 700–600 BCE
Green stone; 5 ¾ × 3 ¼ × ¾ in. (14.5 × 8.2 × 2 cm)
London, The Wyvern Collection, 2074
Page 40, figure 4

Amulet with the demon Lamashtu
Neo-Assyrian, 900–600 BCE
Obsidian; 1 ⅝ × 1 ½ × ¼ in. (4.3 × 3.8 × 0.7 cm)
Paris, Musée du Louvre, Département des Antiquités
orientales, AO 8184
Page 43, figure 7

Amulet with the demon Pazuzu
Neo-Assyrian, 681–627 BCE
Chalcedony; 4 ¾ × 2 ¾ × 3 ½ in. (12 × 7 × 9 cm)
London, The Wyvern Collection, 2048
Page 42, figure 6

Tablet with ritual to counteract witchcraft (*Maqlû*)
Neo-Assyrian, 669–631 BCE
Clay; 8 × 5 ¼ × 1 ⅛ in. (20.3 × 13.3 × 3 cm)
From Nineveh (Kouyunjik), Iraq
London, The British Museum, K.2950
Page 35, figure 1

GREECE

Calyx-krater with Odysseus and Circe
Greek, made in Athens, about 440 BCE, attributed to
the Persephone Painter
Terracotta; 14 ¼ × 14 in. (36.2 × 35.5 cm)
New York, The Metropolitan Museum of Art, Gift of
Amelia E. White, 1941, 41.83
Page 48, figure 1

Fragment of a sarcophagus with Medea
Roman, about 130 CE
Marble; 19 ½ × 33 ½ × 3 ¾ in. (49.5 × 85.1 × 9.5 cm)
Toledo Museum of Art, Orion Fund, 2005.320
Page 8, figure 2

Hydria with Medea and Pelias
Greek, made in Athens, 510–500 BCE, attributed to the
Leagros Group
Terracotta; height: 17 ¼ in. (43.8 cm), diameter at
widest point: 10 ¼ in. (26 cm)
From Vulci, Italy
London, The British Museum, purchased from
Alexandrine Bonaparte, Princess of Canino, through
James Millingen, 1843,1103.59
Page 50, figure 4

Mirror with Medea offering a potion to Jason
Etruscan, about 400 BCE
Bronze; height: 10 in. (25.4 cm), diameter: 7 ¼ in.
(18.3 cm)
London, The British Museum, purchased through
Dr. F. Mayer, 1909,0618.1
Page 49, figure 3

Miniature coffin with curse figure
Greek, 4th century BCE
Lead; 4 ½ × 2 ⅛ × 1 ⅜ in. (11.5 × 5.5 × 3.5 cm)
From the Kerameikos, Athens
Brussels, Musées Royaux d'Art et d'Histoire /
Koninklijke Musea voor Kunst en Geschiedenis,
A.2958
Page 55, figure 7

THE ROMAN EMPIRE

Statuette of triple-bodied Hekate
Roman, 1st–2nd centuries CE
Marble; height: 12 in. (30.5 cm)
New York, The Metropolitan Museum of Art,
The Bothmer Purchase Fund, 1987, 1987.11.2
Page 75, plate 1

Pendant amulet against the evil eye
Roman, 2nd century CE
Gold, pearls, and amethyst; 1 ¼ × ¾ in. (3.1 × 1.8 cm)
Baltimore, Johns Hopkins Archaeological Museum,
485 (formerly FIC.07.225)
Page 76, plate 2

Mummy portrait of a youth wearing an amulet
Egyptian, 150–200 CE
Encaustic on linden wood; 8 × 5 ⅛ in. (20.3 × 13 cm)
Malibu, California, The J. Paul Getty Museum,
Villa Collection, 78.AP.262
Page 79, plate 3

Womb amulet and case
Roman, 1st century CE
Gold; 1 ⅛ × ⅜ in. (2.9 × 1 cm)
Said to be from Beirut, Lebanon
Paris, Bibliothèque nationale de France, Médailles et
Antiques, Inv.56.286–87
Page 80, plate 4

Jewish amulet invoking angels
Roman, 3rd century CE
Silver; 1 ¹¹⁄₁₆ × 2 ¹³⁄₁₆ in. (4.3 × 7.1 cm)
Malibu, California, The J. Paul Getty Museum,
Villa Collection, 80.AM.55.2
Page 81, plate 5

Amulet to influence a legal case
Roman, 4th century CE
Gold; 3 ⅛ × 1 ¹¹⁄₁₆ in. (7.9 × 4.3 cm)
From Bostra (Bosra), Syria
Baltimore, The Walters Art Museum, Gift of the
children of Robert Garrett, 1964, 57.1960
Page 83, plate 7

A priest's handbook of spells ("The London Magical
Papyrus")
Egyptian, 3rd century CE
Papyrus and ink; 33 ¾ × 9 ½ in. (85.7 × 24.3 cm)
From Thebes, Egypt
London, The British Museum, purchased from
Giovanni Anastasi, EA10070,2
Pages 62–63, figure 2

Encrypted magical papyrus
Egyptian, 2nd century CE
Papyrus and ink; 8 ¼ × 11 ⅜ in. (21 × 29 cm)
Ann Arbor, University of Michigan Library
(Papyrology Collection), P.Mich.inv. 534
Page 61, figure 1

Magical papyrus with rituals addressed to Hekate
Egyptian, late 3rd–early 4th centuries CE
Papyrus and ink; 6 × 5 ½ in. (15.2 × 14.2 cm)
Ann Arbor, University of Michigan Library
(Papyrology Collection), P.Mich.inv. 7
Page 84, plate 8

Papyrus with a magician's monologue
Egyptian, 2nd–3rd centuries CE
Papyrus and ink; 3 ¾ × 6 ⅜ in. (8.5 × 16.2 cm)
Ann Arbor, University of Michigan Library
(Papyrology Collection), P.Mich.inv. 5
Page 87, plate 9

Papyrus amulet against fever
Egyptian, 3rd century CE
Papyrus and ink; 4 ¾ × 2 ¼ in. (12 × 5.8 cm)
Ann Arbor, University of Michigan Library
(Papyrology Collection), P.Mich.inv. 6666
Page 64, figure 3

Tablet with homoerotic love charm
Roman, 3rd–4th centuries CE
Lead; 7 × 7 ⅞ in. (18 × 20 cm)
From Hermopolis (El-Ashmunein), Egypt
Florence, Biblioteca Medicea Laurenziana, PSI I.28
Page 65, figure 4

Love charm for four women
Roman, 3rd century CE
Lead; 5 ⅜ × 6 ⅜ in. (13.7 × 16.2 cm)
Said to be from Tunisia
Malibu, California, The J. Paul Getty Museum,
Villa Collection, Gift of Stefan Hornak, 83.AI.244
Page 65, figure 5

Magical gem with the god Mios
Roman, 2nd–3rd centuries CE
Red jasper; diameter at widest point: ¹¹⁄₁₆ in. (1.7 cm)
Said to be from Saqqara, Egypt
The Brooklyn Museum, Charles Edwin Wilbour Fund,
37.1755E
Page 88, plate 10

Magical gem with Osiris
Roman, 2nd–3rd centuries CE
Lapis lazuli; diameter at widest point: ¾ in. (1.9 cm)
Ann Arbor, University of Michigan, Kelsey Museum of
Archaeology, 1963.04.0002
Page 89, plate 11

Magical gem with Serapis
Roman, 2nd–3rd centuries CE
Jasper; diameter at widest point: ⅞ in. (2.3 cm)
Ann Arbor, University of Michigan, Kelsey Museum of
Archaeology, 0000.02.6072
Page 89, plate 12

Magical gem with Harpocrates on solar boat
Roman, 2nd–3rd centuries CE
Hematite; diameter at widest point: 1 in. (2.6 cm)
Ann Arbor, University of Michigan, Kelsey Museum of
Archaeology, 0000.02.6109
Page 90, plate 13

Magical gem with Osiris, Isis, and Nephthys
Roman, 2nd–3rd centuries CE
Bloodstone in gold mount; diameter at widest point:
1 ⅛ in. (2.8 cm)
Ann Arbor, University of Michigan Library (Special
Collections Research Center), SCL-Bonner 56
Page 91, plate 14

Magical gem with Chnoubis
Roman, 2nd–3rd centuries CE
Green chalcedony; diameter at widest point: ⅝ in.
(1.6 cm)
Ann Arbor, University of Michigan, Kelsey Museum of
Archaeology, 0000.02.6009
Page 68, figure 8

Magical gem with double-headed deity
Roman, 2nd–3rd centuries CE
Hematite; diameter at widest point: ¹⁵⁄₁₆ in. (2.4 cm)
Ann Arbor, University of Michigan, Kelsey Museum of
Archaeology, 0000.02.6059
Page 66, figure 6

Magical gem with Harpocrates and the womb
Roman, 2nd–3rd centuries CE
Carnelian; diameter at widest point: 1 ⅛ in. (2.9 cm)
Ann Arbor, University of Michigan Library (Special
Collections Research Center), SCL-Bonner 19
Page 92, plate 15

Magical gem with lizard
Roman, 2nd–3rd centuries CE
Green chalcedony; diameter at widest point: ½ in.
(1.2 cm)
Malibu, California, The J. Paul Getty Museum,
Villa Collection, 81.AN.11.1
Page 94, plate 16

Magical gem with cow-headed Hekate
Roman, 2nd–3rd centuries CE
Black jasper; diameter at widest point: 1 ⅝ in. (4.1 cm)
Ann Arbor, University of Michigan, Kelsey Museum of
Archaeology, 0000.02.6055
Page 67, figure 7

Magical gem with snake-legged deity
Roman, 2nd–3rd centuries CE
Green and red jasper; diameter at widest point: 1 ½ in.
(3.7 cm)
Ann Arbor, University of Michigan, Kelsey Museum of
Archaeology, 0000.02.6054
Page 69, figure 9

Magical gem with lion
Roman, 2nd–3rd centuries CE
Rock crystal; diameter at widest point: ⅞ in. (2.3 cm)
Ann Arbor, University of Michigan, Kelsey Museum of
Archaeology, 0000.02.6050
Page 96, plate 18

Magical gem with Herakles and the Nemean Lion
Roman, 2nd–3rd centuries CE
Red jasper; diameter at widest point: 1 ¾ in. (4.5 cm)
Paris, Bibliothèque nationale de France, Médailles et
Antiques, Inv.58.2220bis
Page 97, plate 19

Curse tablet
Roman, 3rd century CE
Selenite; 3 ½ × 5 ½ in. (8.9 ×14 cm)
From Amathous (Ayios Tychonas), Cyprus
London, The British Museum, purchased from
Captain G. Hancock, 1890, 1891,0418.50
Page 98, plate 20

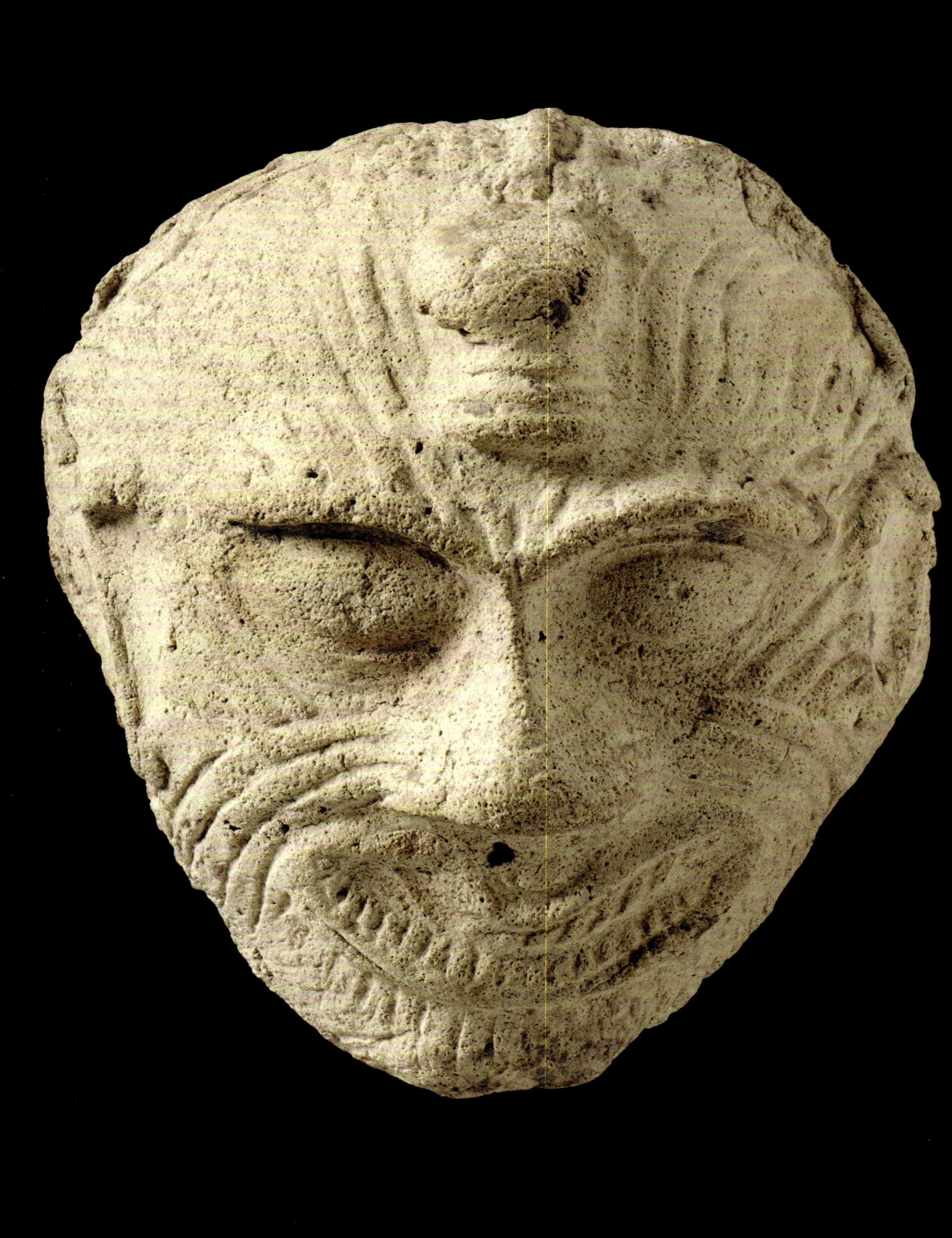

Further Reading

EGYPT

Borghouts, J. F., trans. *Ancient Egyptian Magical Texts.* E. J. Brill, 1978.

Quirke, Stephen. *Exploring Religion in Ancient Egypt.* Wiley-Blackwell, 2015.

Riggs, Christina. *Ancient Egyptian Magic: A Hands-On Guide.* Thames & Hudson, 2020.

Ritner, Robert Kriech. *The Mechanics of Ancient Egyptian Magical Practice.* The Oriental Institute of the University of Chicago, 1993.

MESOPOTAMIA

Abusch, Tzvi. *The Witchcraft Series Maqlû.* Society of Biblical Literature, 2015.

Wisnom, Selena. *The Library of Ancient Wisdom: Mesopotamia and the Making of the Modern World.* University of Chicago Press, 2025.

GREECE AND ROME

Betz, Hans Dieter, ed. *The Greek Magical Papyri in Translation Including the Demotic Spells.* 2nd ed. University of Chicago Press, 1992.

Dickie, Matthew. *Magic and Magicians in the Greco-Roman World.* Routledge, 2001.

Dieleman, Jacco. *Priests, Tongues, and Rites: The London-Leiden Magical Manuscripts and Translation in Egyptian Ritual (100–300 CE).* Brill, 2005.

Faraone, Christopher A. *Ancient Greek Love Magic.* Harvard University Press, 1999.

Faraone, Christopher A. *The Transformation of Greek Amulets in Roman Imperial Times.* University of Pennsylvania Press, 2018.

Gager, John G., ed. *Curse Tablets and Binding Spells from the Ancient World.* Oxford University Press, 1992.

Kotanksy, Roy. *Greek Magical Amulets: The Inscribed Gold, Silver, Copper, and Bronze Lamellae; Part I: Published Texts of Known Provenance.* Westdeutscher Verlag, 1994.

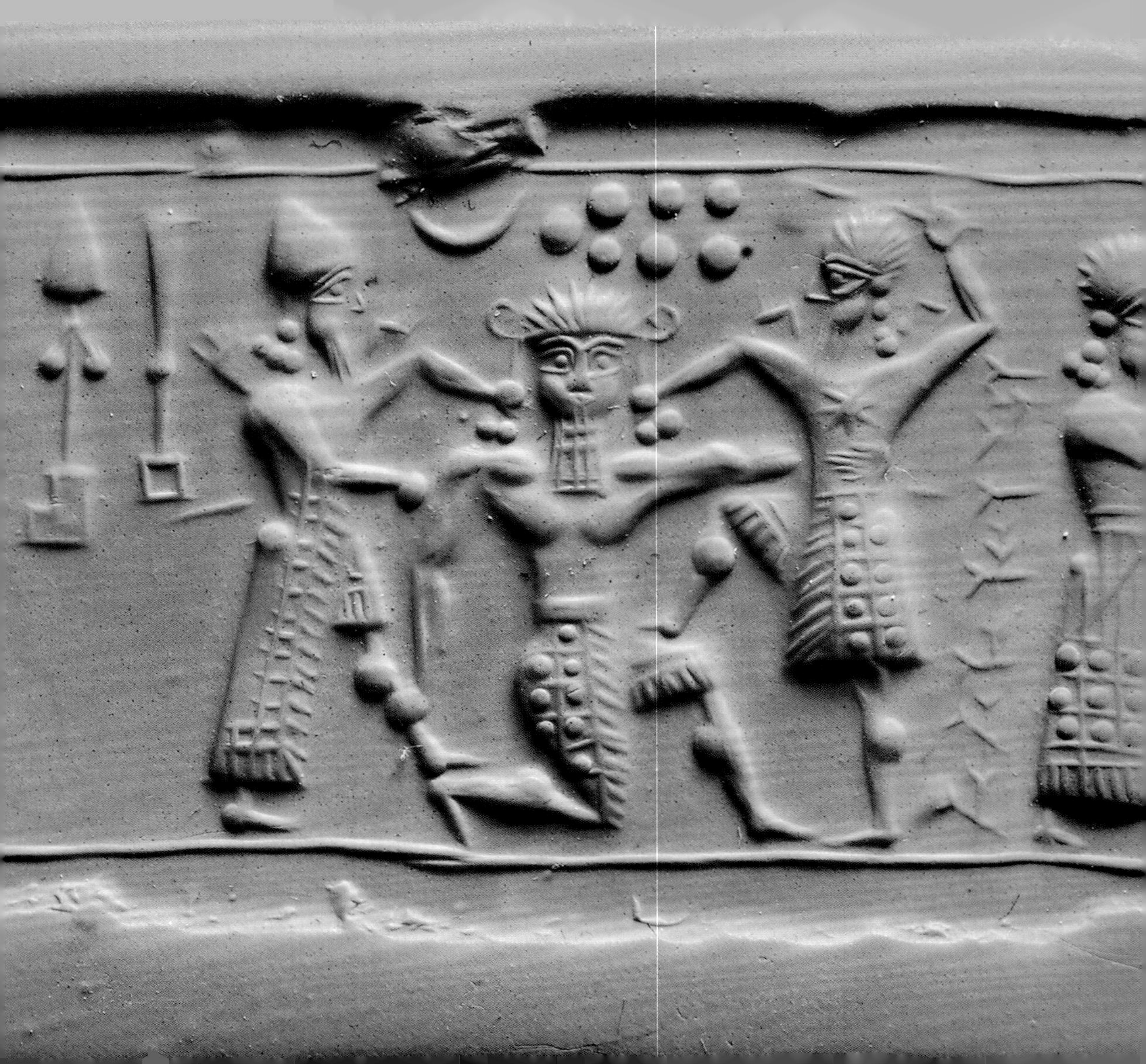

Contributors

JEFFREY SPIER completed his DPhil at Merton College, Oxford, and taught classical archaeology at University College London and the University of Arizona before joining the Getty Museum as Senior Curator of Antiquities in 2014. He has published on many aspects of Greek art and iconography, gems and jewelry, numismatics, early Christian and Byzantine art, ancient magic, and the history of collecting. His books include *Ancient Gems and Finger Rings: Catalogue of the Collections, The J. Paul Getty Museum*; *Late Antique and Early Christian Gems*; *Picturing the Bible: The Earliest Christian Art*; and *Late Byzantine Rings, 1204–1453*. He has organized a number of important exhibitions and catalogues at the Getty, including *Beyond the Nile: Egypt and the Classical World* (with Timothy Potts and Sara E. Cole); *Persia: Ancient Iran and the Classical World* (with Timothy Potts and Sara E. Cole); and *Ancient Thrace and the Classical World: Treasures from Bulgaria, Romania, and Greece* (with Timothy Potts, Sara E. Cole, and Margarit Damyanov). He also curated and edited *Rubens: Picturing Antiquity* (with Anne Woollett and Davide Gasparotto). He retired from the Getty in early 2024.

GINA KONSTANTOPOULOS is an associate professor in Assyriology and cuneiform studies in the Department of Near Eastern Languages and Cultures at the University of California, Los Angeles. Her research centers on religion, magic, and literature in Mesopotamia, with a focus on the role of demons and monsters. She is the author of *The Divine/Demonic Seven and the Place of Demons in Mesopotamia*. Her current research is on the creation of distant and imagined lands and notions of space and place in the ancient Near East, particularly the intersection of distant space and empire in the first millennium BCE. She holds a PhD in Near Eastern studies from the University of Michigan.

FOY SCALF is Head of the Research Archives at the Institute for the Study of Ancient Cultures of the University of Chicago, where he also leads the Integrated Database Project. An Egyptologist with a PhD from the University of Chicago, he researches the intersection of ancient Egyptian intellectual culture, textual transmission, and the history of the book, with a focus on orality, close textual analysis, and religious practice. He curated the acclaimed exhibition *Book of the Dead: Becoming God in Ancient Egypt* and edited its scholarly catalogue. Scalf is principal investigator on several digital humanities projects, including the CEDAR Book of the Dead project and the ISAC Demotic Ostraca Online database.

Photography Credits

Page 6: Courtesy Toledo Museum of Art Archives; **page 8:** Courtesy Toledo Museum of Art; **page 16:** © RMN-Grand Palais / Art Resource, NY, © Christian Décamps; **page 17:** Courtesy Leipzig University Library; **page 18, fig. 3:** © The Metropolitan Museum of Art / Art Resource, NY; **page 18, fig. 4:** Courtesy Johns Hopkins Archaeological Museum, photography by Will Kirk; **pages 19–20:** © The Metropolitan Museum of Art / Art Resource, NY; **page 21:** © Georges Poncet / Dist. RMN-Grand Palais / Art Resource, NY; **page 22:** © The Metropolitan Museum of Art / Art Resource, NY; **page 23, fig. 9:** Courtesy Foy D. Scalf; **page 23, fig. 10:** Courtesy Image Studio, Royal Museums of Art and History, Brussels; **pages 24–25, fig. 11:** Courtesy Brooklyn Museum; **page 25, fig. 12:** Courtesy Petrie Museum of Egyptian and Sudanese Archaeology, University College London; **page 26:** Courtesy of the Institute for the Study of Ancient Cultures of the University of Chicago; **page 27:** Courtesy Walters Art Museum; **page 28:** © The Metropolitan Museum of Art / Art Resource, NY; **page 29, fig. 16:** Courtesy of the Institute for the Study of Ancient Cultures of the University of Chicago; **page 29, fig. 17:** © The Metropolitan Museum of Art / Art Resource, NY; **page 30:** Robert K. Ritner, courtesy of the Institute for the Study of Ancient Cultures of the University of Chicago; **pages 35, 38, 39:** © The Trustees of the British Museum; **page 40:** Private collection, UK; **page 41:** © Musée du Louvre, Dist. RMN-Grand Palais / Thierry Olivier / Art Resource, NY; **page 42:** Private collection, UK; **page 43:** © Musée du Louvre, Dist. RMN-Grand Palais / Thierry Olivier; **page 48, fig. 1:** © The Metropolitan Museum of Art / Art Resource, NY; **page 48, fig. 2:** © 2026 Museum of Fine Arts, Boston; **pages 49–50:** © The Trustees of the British Museum; **page 51:** © Photographic Archive, National Archaeological Museum of Naples; **page 54:** © 2026 Museum of Fine Arts, Boston; **page 55:** Courtesy Image Studio, Royal Museums of Art and History, Brussels; **page 56:** Courtesy Beinecke Rare Book and Manuscript Library, Yale University, photography by Deon Griffin; **page 61:** Courtesy University of Michigan Library, Papyrology Collection; **pages 62–63:** © The Trustees of the British Museum; **page 64:** Courtesy University of Michigan Library, Papyrology Collection; **page 65, fig. 4:** Reproduced with permission of the Italian Ministry of Culture; **page 65, fig. 5:** Courtesy J. Paul Getty Museum; **pages 66–69:** Courtesy Kelsey Museum of Archaeology, University of Michigan; **page 75:** © The Metropolitan Museum of Art / Art Resource, NY; **page 76:** Courtesy Johns Hopkins Archaeological Museum; **page 79:** Digital image courtesy of Getty's Open Content Program; **page 80:** Courtesy Bibliothèque nationale de France; **page 81:** Courtesy J. Paul Getty Museum; **page 82:** Courtesy Symbolic & Chase; **page 83:** Courtesy Walters Art Museum; **pages 84, 87:** Courtesy University of Michigan Library, Papyrology Collection; **page 88:** Courtesy Brooklyn Museum; **pages 89–90:** Courtesy Kelsey Museum of Archaeology, University of Michigan; **pages 91, 92:** Courtesy University of Michigan Library (Special Collections Research Center); **page 94:** Courtesy J. Paul Getty Museum; **page 95:** © The Metropolitan Museum of Art / Art Resource, NY; **page 96:** Courtesy Kelsey Museum of Archaeology, University of Michigan; **page 97:** Courtesy Bibliothèque nationale de France; **page 98:** © The Trustees of the British Museum

This book was made possible with the assistance of the Andrew W. Mellon Foundation.

Published in conjunction with the exhibition *Cursed! The Power of Magic in the Ancient World*, organized by the Toledo Museum of Art, Toledo, Ohio, March 21–July 5, 2026.

Cursed! The Power of Magic in the Ancient World is made possible through the generous support of Presenting Sponsors Susan and Tom Palmer, Season Sponsor Taylor Automotive Family, and Silver Sponsors Edward W. and Barnwell E. Lane III, Toledo Museum of Art Ambassadors, the Rita Barbour Kern Foundation, and the Ohio Arts Council, which receives support from the State of Ohio and the National Endowment for the Arts.

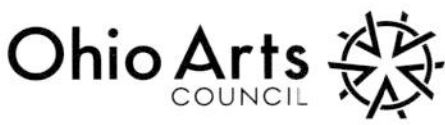

First published in the United States of America in 2026 by

Toledo Museum of Art
2445 Monroe Street
Toledo, OH 43620
www.toledomuseum.org
Tel. 419 255 8000

Available through:
ARTBOOK | D.A.P.
75 Broad Street, Suite 630
New York, NY 10004
www.artbook.com

ISBN: 978-1-64657-050-8

Editor and Publications Manager: Stephanie Rozman
Imaging Specialist: Julia Hayes

Produced by Marquand Books, Seattle
   www.marquandbooks.com
Designed by Ryan Polich
Typeset by Tina Henderson
Proofread by Bruno George
Color management by I/O Color, Seattle
Printed and bound in China by C&C Offset
   Printing Co., Inc.

This publication is the culmination of work by individuals across the Toledo Museum of Art and beyond. We extend our gratitude to Edward Drummond and Florence Scott Libbey President, Director, and CEO Adam Levine; Deputy Director Andrea Gardner; Assistant Curator of Ancient Art Roko Rumora; and the following TMA staff for their contributions: Vanessa Applebaum, Gabriela Carlos, Nate Coryell, Emily Croak, Emily Cummins, Candice Dunn, Vivian Fitzgerald, Pamela Goldsmith, Julia Hayes, Julie Hayter, Anna Johnson, Adero Kauffmann-Okoko, Libbey Koppinger, Anna Marley, Greer Mehler, Ali Moser, Lori Mott, Annabelle Nolasco, Heidi Orth, Patricia O'Toole, Amy Passiak, Paula Reich, Stephanie Rozman, Mary Sabin, Marissa Stevenson, Jannell Swisher, and Ellen Wise.

Cover illustration: Magical gem with snake-legged deity (reverse), Roman, 2nd–3rd centuries CE. Kelsey Museum of Archaeology, 0000.02.6054. Page 69, figure 9. Image courtesy Kelsey Museum of Archaeology, University of Michigan. **Page 2:** Amulet with the demon Pazuzu, Neo-Assyrian, 681–627 BCE. The Wyvern Collection, 2048. Page 42, figure 6. Image courtesy private collection, UK. **Page 4:** Calyx-krater with Odysseus and Circe, Greek, made in Athens, about 440 BCE, attributed to the Persephone Painter. The Metropolitan Museum of Art, Gift of Amelia E. White, 1941, 41.83. Page 48, figure 1. Image © The Metropolitan Museum of Art / Art Resource, NY. **Page 10:** Amulet with the demon Lamashtu, Neo-Assyrian, 700–600 BCE. The Wyvern Collection, 2074. Page 40, figure 4. Image courtesy private collection, UK. **Page 100:** Statuette of triple-bodied Hekate (detail), Roman, 1st–2nd centuries CE. The Metropolitan Museum of Art, The Bothmer Purchase Fund, 1987, 1987.11.2. Page 75, plate 1. Image © The Metropolitan Museum of Art / Art Resource, NY. **Page 106:** Mask of Humbaba, Old Babylonian, 2000–1700 BCE. The British Museum, 1931,1010.458. Page 39, figure 3. Image © The Trustees of the British Museum. **Page 108:** Cylinder seal depicting Gilgamesh and Enkidu slaying Humbaba (detail), Neo-Assyrian, 8th century BCE. The British Museum, 1868,0616.1. Page 38, figure 2. Image © The Trustees of the British Museum.

About the typefaces: Albertus Nova was designed by Berthold Wolpe and digitized/updated by Toshi Omagari, Fazeta was designed by Andrej Dieneš, Nocturne Serif was designed by Mateusz Machalski, and Infini was designed by Sandrine Nugue as part of a public commission by the Centre national des arts plastiques.